MW01630866

Remington's Vest Pocket Pistols

by Robert E. Hatfield

ANDREW MOWBRAY PUBLISHERS • P.O. BOX 460 • LINCOLN, RI 02865 USA

LIBRARY OF CONGRESS
CATALOG CARD NO. 01-135474
Remington's Vest Pocket Pistols
Lincoln, R.I.: Andrew Mowbray Incorporated — Publishers
120 pp.

ISBN: 0-917218-98-1

To order more copies of this book call 1-800-999-4697.

Printed in the United States of America.

This book was designed and set in type by Jo-Ann Langlois.

On the Front Cover —

Remington Vest Pocket Pistols in each of the four calibers manufactured: (Right) No. 1 Size, .22 caliber rimfire, blue finish, rosewood grips, SN4146; (center) No. 2 Size, .30 caliber rimfire, brass frame, blue barrel, walnut grips, SN433; (top) No. 2 Size, factory engraved, .32 caliber rimfire in the white, with vertically grained walnut grips, SN191; (bottom) No. 3 Size, .41 caliber rimfire, nickel frame, blue barrel, ivory grips, SN2037.
(Author's collection; photo by Nick Decker, Lake Ozark, MO)

1 2 3 4 5 6 7 8 9 10

This book is dedicated to the memory of Eliphalet Remington, his descendants and successors, the employees of Remington and to the members of the Remington Society of America past and present. And, especially to the numerous collectors involved in the continuing research of things Remington. This endeavor was undertaken to promote better understanding of the development, production and distribution of the Remington Vest Pocket Pistols.

With Special Thanks

to those Great Collectors of Remington's Vest Pocket Pistols who responded to the surveys and assisted in so many other ways.

About the Author

Colonel Robert E. (Bob) Hatfield, retired with more than 33 years of service with the U.S. Army Artillery, (Active Army, National Guard and Army Reserve combined.)

His military education includes: The Army General School, Ft. Riley, Kansas; The Basic and the Advanced Field Artillery Officer Courses and The Nuclear Weapons Officer Course, at Ft. Sill, Oklahoma; Command and General Staff College, Ft. Leavenworth, Kansas; The Industrial College of the Armed Forces and the Air War College.

An avid gun collector for more than 50 years, the author published a monograph, "Remington Vest Pocket Pistol and the Celebrated Saw-Handle-Grip Pistol," in September of 1997.

His "Remington Vest Pocket Pistol Serial Number Story" was presented in a *Remington Society of America Journal* article, 2nd Quarter 1999. In the 1st Quarter *RSA Journal* "Remington Firearms Research" he suggested collectors get involved in research.

Hatfield is a member/director of the Remington Society of America and serves as that organization's Merchandise Manager. An NRA member, he is also a member of the Ohio Gun Collector's Association, Missouri Valley Arms Collectors Association and a life member of the Veterans of Foreign Wars. Hatfield attended Shurtleff College, Alton, Illinois, and Washington University, St. Louis, Missouri.

He has retired from an advertising career that culminated as Executive Vice-President and Director of the Toyota Retail Division with the firm of Saatchi and Saatchi.

Since his several retirements, Hatfield's volunteer endeavors have included the Lake of the Ozarks Jazz Festivals, Lake Area Chamber of Commerce Board of Directors, Easter Seals Drives, Special Olympics Bowl-a-thons, Kiwanis Club charity efforts, local area fund-raising drives and Salvation Army Christmas bell ringing.

Bob has a son and two daughters, seven grandchildren, and is an Elder of the Lake Ozark Christian Church. He resides at the Lake of the Ozarks in the heart of Missouri.

Table of Contents

Introduction

For me, fascination with firearms started when I acquired a Spencer Safety Hammerless, .22 caliber short, five-shot revolver. Twelve years old and full of curiosity, I just had to know everything there was to know about this rimfire marvel. The Jennie B. Hayner Public Library in Alton, Illinois, really didn't have much of a selection in its "Gun Publication" section. References were subsequently found identifying such a pistol having been produced in .32 caliber only. (Just last year I read somewhere that "just maybe" Spencer "could have" produced their Hammerless Revolver in .22 caliber. They must have produced at least one .22 caliber model, 'cause I still have one.)

More than fifty years later, at the June 1996 Lake of the Ozarks/Bagnell Dam Gun Show (sponsored by the local Lions Club), I purchased a .22 caliber (rimfire short) Remington Vest Pocket Pistol. That old curiosity surfaced one more time, as it has numerous other times through the years. Remembering a couple of articles in the *Remington Society of America (RSA) Journal* by Ol' RemShots (a.k.a. Leon Wier), I phoned the President of RSA (same person, just another a.k.a.) to learn everything there was to know about Remington Vest Pocket Pistols.

When he was asked who was doing (or had done) significant research on Remington Vest Pocket Pistols, Ol' RemShots replied that he knew of no one. "Why don't you undertake this?" He added, "This might be a good project for you!"

This led to the preparation of the 1997 monograph, entitled "Remington's Vest Pocket Pistol and the Celebrated Saw-Handle-Grip Pocket Pistol." As I have explained in that initial research documentation attempt, "...like an eager teenager seeking favor from a teacher, I jumped right in and accepted his challenge."

Late in October 1996, draft copies of the initial "Research Survey Form" were sent to Ol' RemShots and to the *RSA Journal* editor, Roy Marcot. Leon suggested some constructive alterations. Roy very graciously inserted copies of the form in the next issue of the *Journal*.

Numerous completed forms were received. (Remington collectors are the greatest!) I was truly surprised with the volume of immediate responses. Information received was reviewed and recorded on a computer spreadsheet. Data was collated and tabulated. Charts were designed. By August 1, 1997, a draft of the September 1997 monograph had been sent to the printer.

This obvious "Rush to Publication" was self-serving. I was about to travel to Cody, Wyoming, where the Remington Society was meeting. Remington collectors and enthusiasts from all over were going to be there. A hundred or so copies were taken to the society meeting and were given to the members present at that seminar. Each person in attendance got a copy of his/her very own. (Here's the self-serving part — Who better to critique any effort on anything Remington than Remington collectors, many of them experienced gun book authors.)

Again, the response was terrific. One of the attendees shared his copy with Herbert G. Houze. His book review in *Man at Arms* magazine (Vol. 20, No. 1, Jan./Feb. 1998) prompted submission of more completed research forms as well as requests for copies of the monograph. Thank you, Mr. Houze.

When the initial distribution of the research survey form was made, the cooperative spirit of Remington collectors became very apparent. Some made copies of the form and gave (sent) them to friends and colleagues, encouraging them to get involved and share their Remington Vest Pocket Pistol information.

Copies of early Remington advertising and reprints of Remington catalog items were voluntarily submitted with research forms. Photographs of individual Vest Pockets were sent. Offers to assist in any way possible, notes of encouragement, and best wishes for success in the research effort were received.

Throughout this project the assistance I received was remarkable. Not only had the requested information been provided, but suggestions for improvement of the form were received. They have really helped. On the initial survey form was the invitation to offer "...suggestions on improvement of this form, etc." Respondents were not only willing but eager to help.

Among the suggestions received were the following:

1. Location of markings is needed.
2. Direction of the markings (reading breech-to-muzzle or muzzle-to-breech).
3. Clarify whether the respondent is to count the grip screw, or not, in the pin and screw count.
4. Request photographs of Remington Vest Pocket Pistols, and explain that pictures could not be returned.
5. Ask permission to use their photos in future publications...and subsequent to receiving that permission, recognize contributors in print if and when their pictures are used.
6. Include a space for the date the form was completed, which will make revised submissions easier to recognize.
7. Include my own phone number, fax number and e-mail address to make it easier for people to take part in the survey.
8. Illustrate a definite method to measure barrel lengths.
9. Add spaces for the respondent's phone and fax numbers and e-mail addresses.

Remington's Vest Pocket Pistol and the Celebrated Saw-Handle-Grip Pocket Pistol, by Robert Hatfield. Robert Hatfield, P.O. Box 586, Lake Ozark, MO 65049-0586. 17 pp.; 5⅜" x 8½"; 2 b&w ill.; paperback. $5.00 (plus $1.00 p/h)

In a way, it is appropriate that the size of this pamphlet mirrors that of its subject. Yet, despite its diminutiveness, *Remington's Vest Pocket Pistol* contains some valuable information.

Using data secured during a nationwide survey, Hatfield has reconstructed the estimated serial number ranges and probable production figures for the four calibers of Vest Pocket Pistols manufactured by E. Remington & Sons. In addition, he has collated the general specifications for the model (Table 3).

From a collector's standpoint, it is likely that the individual characteristic tables Hatfield has assembled for each caliber type will prove to be the most used section of this little book. In these, he presents the statistical breakdowns of finish and grip types, presence of engraving and barrel lengths encountered. All these features will assist owners in determining the rarity of the pocket pistols they own.

While not a lavish study, monographs such as this one provide a valuable service, and their production should be encouraged.

H.G.H.

Consequently, the Research Survey Form was revised. Copies of the updated form were again sent to Leon Wier and Roy Marcot for review. The revised form was included in the next mailing of the *Remington Society of America Journal*. (Copies of all three Remington Vest Pocket Pistol Research Survey Forms used in this project are included in the "Research Techniques" Section.)

Many new submissions plus numerous revised contributions came in. The updating process was underway. A significant portion of the serial numbers included in this research were furnished by many other Remington enthusiasts. People who have, over the years, been observing and recording them at gun shows, museums and in various gun publications shared their findings. Their efforts have helped immensely to expand the scope of this research.

Joseph Rider's Parlor Pistol...

Let's Take a Moment For Historical Review

The strange looking pistol pictured here is an ancestor of the Remington Vest Pocket Pistol. Sometime in 1859, Joseph Rider developed the "Rider Parlor Pistol." A .17 caliber ball was propelled by using only a percussion cap. No additional gunpowder charge was used. From this little parlor pistol eventually evolved the Remington Vest Pocket Pistol line.

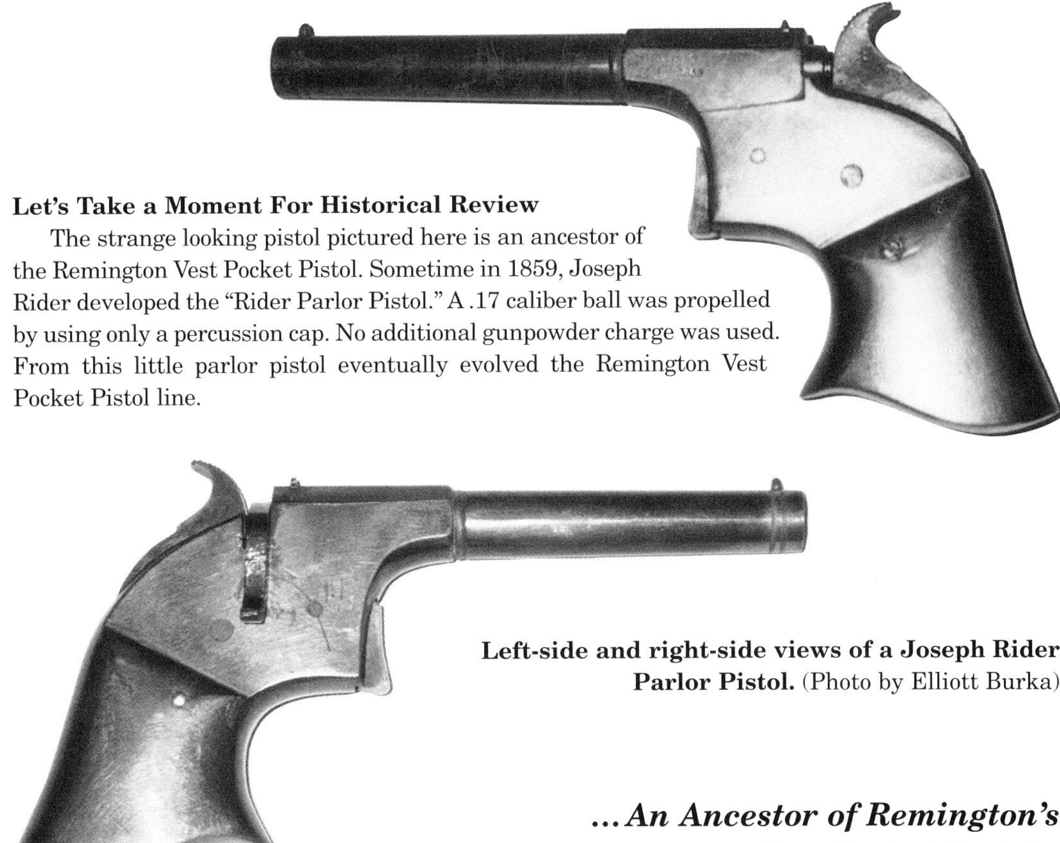

Left-side and right-side views of a Joseph Rider Parlor Pistol. (Photo by Elliott Burka)

...An Ancestor of Remington's Vest Pocket Pistols.

When Remington did start manufacturing their Vest Pocket Pistols, they eventually made them in three different sizes and four different calibers. One of each caliber is illustrated in the photo on page 10.

The most fascinating element I confronted during this research was the myriad of sometimes inconsistent and confusing dialogue along with the misinformation that was supplied about the Remington Vest Pocket Pistol, in .22 caliber (rimfire short), and the Split-Breech Vest Pocket Pistols, in .30 caliber, .32 caliber and .41 caliber (all rimfire short).

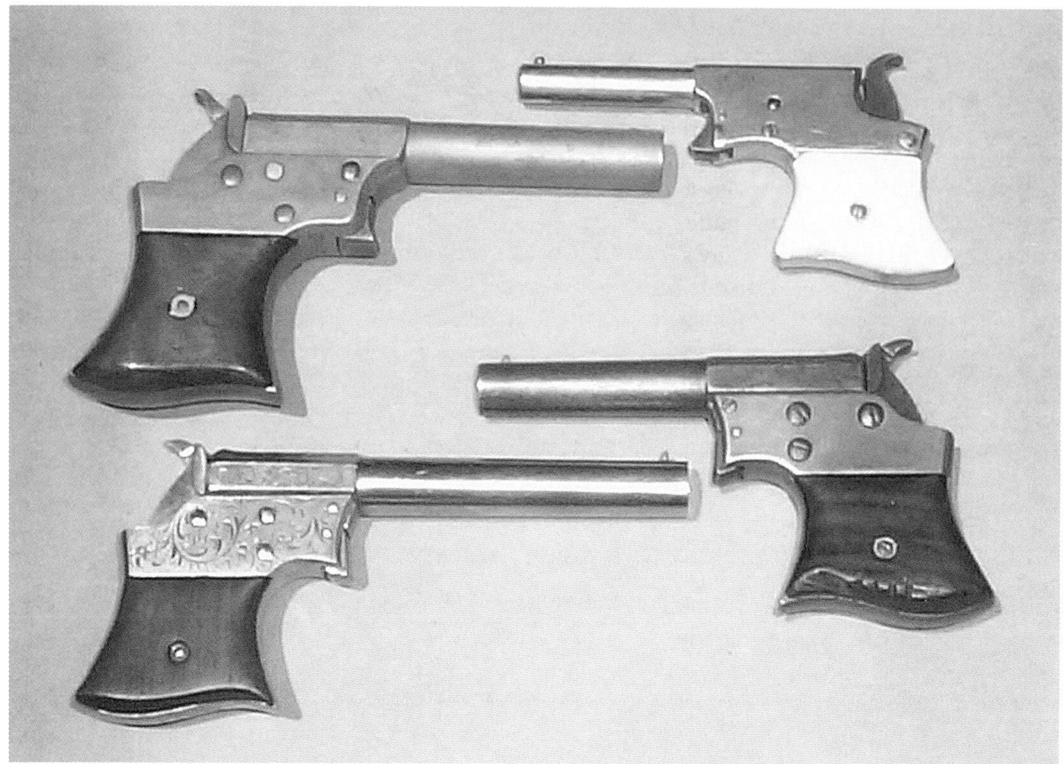

Remington Vest Pocket Pistols (clockwise from upper left): .41 cal. SN2260; .22 cal. SN10178; .30 cal. (brass frame) SN1540; .32 cal. (Factory engraved in the white) SN191.
(All from the Author's Collection)

Regardless of the researcher's motivation (trying to gather information on a single vest pocket pistol or seeking more extensive knowledge of the entire spectrum of Remington Vest Pocket Pistol production), or the level of the individual's firearms knowledge and expertise, one learns quickly that there is no real single source that approaches a reasonably complete publication devoted to the subject of Remington Vest Pocket Pistols.

Much has been written through the years, and numerous photos have been taken and published in a variety of formats. They have included illustrations of some of the most beautiful and well-maintained Remington Vest Pocket Pistols anyone could imagine.

Beyond the enjoyment of just viewing these guns, which most of us can only fantasize about owning, there remains much confusion. For example, the authors of resource do not agree on just when actual production began, nor do they all share similar opinions on what calibers of Vest Pocket Pistols Remington actually manufactured. Many have also expressed opinions that each caliber produced was provided a separate series of serial numbers starting with Number 1. (Subscribing to that theory was easy until the serial number sequence began to "indicate" differently.)

If that were true, duplication of serial numbers should have surfaced after such a large volume of these diminutive weapons were scrutinized and compared. That has not happened. Yet, numerical analysis techniques predict a duplication of serial numbers of significant magnitude.

There is certainly no consensus as to the total number of Remington Vest Pocket Pistols manufactured in each of the four calibers, let alone overall. Until the serial number dilemma is resolved, it will be impossible to make a reasonably accurate estimate of the quantity of Remington Vest Pocket Pistols. Securing information from existing sources isn't too difficult.

The big question remains — How much of it should you rely on as accurate?

There has been much controversy as to what to call these Remington-built single-shot pistols that easily fit into a vest pocket, a muff or even a garter. One source states that Remington referred to the .22 caliber Vest Pocket Pistols as their "No. 1 Size." The .30 and .32 caliber models were called their "No. 2 Size" while the .41 caliber models were referred to as their "No. 3 Size."

There did not appear to be any single and clear-cut proper designation to use to identify these little Remington single-shot pistols, and to maintain this effort as an extension of the study initiated in the September 1997 monograph. This book's title, *Remington's Vest Pocket Pistols* says it all. Hopefully, hereafter, collectors will just simply call them "Remington Vest Pocket Pistols."

After reading everything I could find concerning Remington Vest Pocket Pistols, the information was logged and the findings were compared. Hundreds of these pistols have been observed and/or reported. Details were submitted in response to requests on the research forms. A spreadsheet format was developed to allow for immediate access and ease of comparison.

Numerous collectors, authors (many of whom are members of the Remington Society of America), and museum curators and their staff personnel have tolerated my inquiries. A tremendous volume of communication was involved. The U.S. Postal Service, Internet e-mail, fax machines as well as various telephone service providers were utilized. Facts concerning Remington's Vest Pocket Pistols poured in from every sector.

The Vest Pocket Pistols in my collection have been dismantled. Amazingly enough, they have been reassembled and are still functioning. Their parts have been cleaned and oiled. Illustrations have been drawn of them and they have been photographed. Each and every part has been identified from catalog parts listings when possible. When such identity was not possible, the parts were given the most logical names. Conclusions and assumptions that have been developed as a by-product of this research are shared later in this book.

When you are attempting to find out as much as possible about Remington Vest Pocket Pistols, colorful photographs can be found in any number of publications. (Take a look at the plethora of sources in this book's bibliography.)

While this volume does contain photographs of numerous Remington Vest Pocket Pistols, a sincere attempt has been made to use heretofore unpublished pictures, charts, graphs, drawings and exploded views. You will find illustrations reproduced from old Remington catalogs, including a listing of parts that was utilized to provide proper nomenclature for the parts illustrated. (Ol' RemShots pointed out this source material and provided other guidance, which is truly appreciated.). Copies of old Remington advertisements also appear in this publication.

An arbitrary date of August 31, 1999, was established to end the research to be used to tabulate the research results included in this volume. However, traveling to Ilion, New York, on September 20, 21 and 30, generated such an outpouring of additional information, photographs and material not previously known by the author. Because of the nature of some of the newly acquired knowledge, the decision was made to slow down the process to allow inclusion in this book. The final research closing date was changed to November 30. Even though this volume has been printed, the research continues. Hopefully, there is additional retrievable information out there somewhere. Further undisclosed data could provide confirmation or repudiation of the opinions, assumptions and conclusions expressed herein.

There are still many gaps in the serial number scale. Other Remington catalogs may exist that haven't thus far surfaced. Additional advertising by Remington and/or distributors and gun dealers may be uncovered and shared. Items such as these should provide the verification and validation being sought and be so helpful in unlocking additional secrets concerning Remington Vest Pocket Pistols.

L.W. Moody, from Alum Bridge, West Virginia, a machinist since 1974, really took a liking to the Remington-Rider Parlor Pistol. So much so that he set about to build a reproduction. His advertising brochure explains that Joseph Rider received a patent dated September 13, 1859. Less than 1,000 of the Remington-Rider Parlor Pistols were manufactured, according to Moody, from 1860 to 1863.

Moody's reproductions are full-scale, with 3-inch barrels and weigh from 4 ounces to 4½ ounces. The barrel, frame and grip (on the right side) are one integral brass cast piece, just like the originals were made.

The following illustrations reveal the front page, centerfold (the two interior pages), and the back page of "Moody's Advertising Brochure" describing the Remington Parlor Pistol reproductions that he manufactured.

Early in the research process, I was admonished by a collector in Oklahoma to be extremely diligent concerning accuracy. This was very disturbing, because every facet of documentation had

You'll soon get the impression that you've seen the name "L.W. Moody" somewhere before, probably because pictures of some of his collection are included in this book.

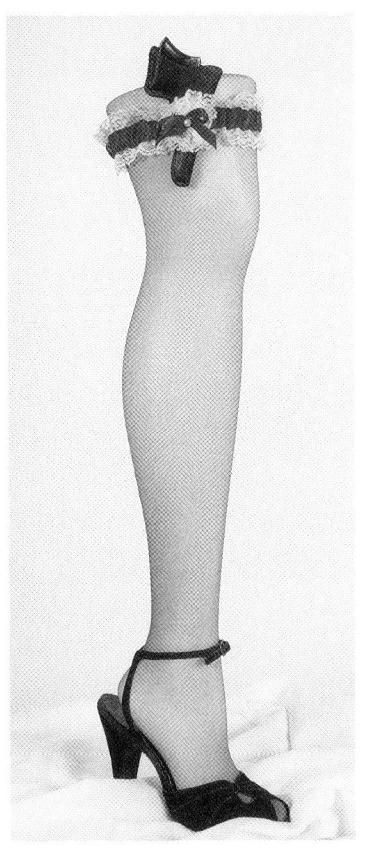

Gun collecting can and should be fun and exciting. Make the most of your Remington collectibles and enjoy them to the fullest. Larry Moody sure seems to really enjoy his. Take a look at the interesting manner in which he displays a holster and one of his Remington Vest Pocket Pistols, SN2268. He tells a great story concerning the acquisition of this leg at a flea market. Maybe we should ask his wife to relate all of the circumstances of that shopping trip!

Remington Vest Pocket Pistol, .22 cal., SN2268 in a leather holster, displayed on a leg!
(RSA member Larry Moody Collection. Photo by Drew Moody)

Vest Pocket Pistol, SN2268 and leather holster.
(RSA member Larry Moody Collection. Photo by Drew Moody)

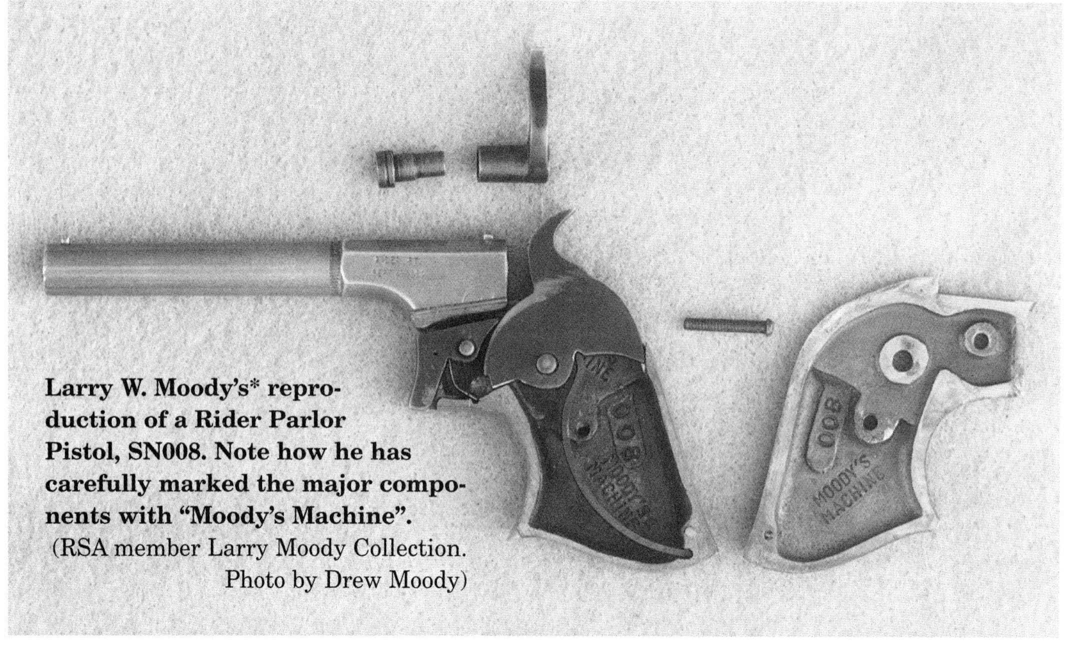

Larry W. Moody's* reproduction of a Rider Parlor Pistol, SN008. Note how he has carefully marked the major components with "Moody's Machine".
(RSA member Larry Moody Collection. Photo by Drew Moody)

been checked and rechecked. This incident occurred after the initial monograph had gone to press in September 1997. It appeared to this gentleman that the printed text was incorrect, because it had not included as many pearl grips as he alone had submitted.

Going back to the submitted research forms, the explanation became immediately clear. Even though the study was dated September 1997, the cut-off date for input to be prepared for the printer was early in August. Any material received after the printer's cut-off date would not have been included. This was the case of some of the information my critic had submitted. During ongoing research, this type of occurrence remains possible. Every precaution has been exercised to assure accuracy throughout this study.

Someone once said, "Copying another's style, design and/or product is the sincerest form of flattery!" Remington should have been quite flattered when European manufacturers built copies of the Vest Pocket Pistols. Every small pistol you run across out there with similar lines to those of the Remington Vest Pocket Pistol isn't necessarily a Remington. Be sure to check as many details and features as possible of the Remington Vest Pocket Pistols so you will know whether or not you have a "Genuine Remington" or somebody else's look-alike.

Take a real close look at the pair of pistols on page 15. These two pistols are *not* Remington Vest Pocket Pistols. Generally similar is all. Their origins are questionable.

Please note that at a glance they do appear very much alike. But a closer look reveals that they are certainly not totally carbon copies. Close but no cigar. Their hammer outlines are different, the positioning of the front sight post is dissimilar, and their grip retaining screws complete with their escutcheons have been placed in different positions.

Also in contrast to the Remington models, the counterfeits each have an outside lever on the left side of their receivers. One of these pistols, probably a European copy of a Remington Vest Pocket Pistol, appears to have four screws (not counting the grip screw) and a single pin, while

---

**Special Note: Larry asked that I include the fact that his Rider Parlor Pistol reproduction, SN007, was stolen from an Ohio Gun Show while it was being displayed on Marv Adam's table.*

the other has three screws and two pins. Their trigger shapes are slightly different. The general shape of their frames and their grip frames differ, also.

The top photograph here was sent to Leon Wier, Jr. (You know, Ol' RemShots) by Robert P. Carter, seeking information. Leon responded (in the 3rd Quarter 1999 *RSA Journal*) with the opinion that it is was not a Remington. I certainly agree.

It is most likely a .22 caliber weapon, since there doesn't appear to be any separate breech mechanism between the hammer and the chamber.

And, just like Ol' RemShots had said, "…it is impossible to ascertain much more about it from the photograph." Being able to see it firsthand, to gauge the bore and inspect the pistol up close, could reveal further information.

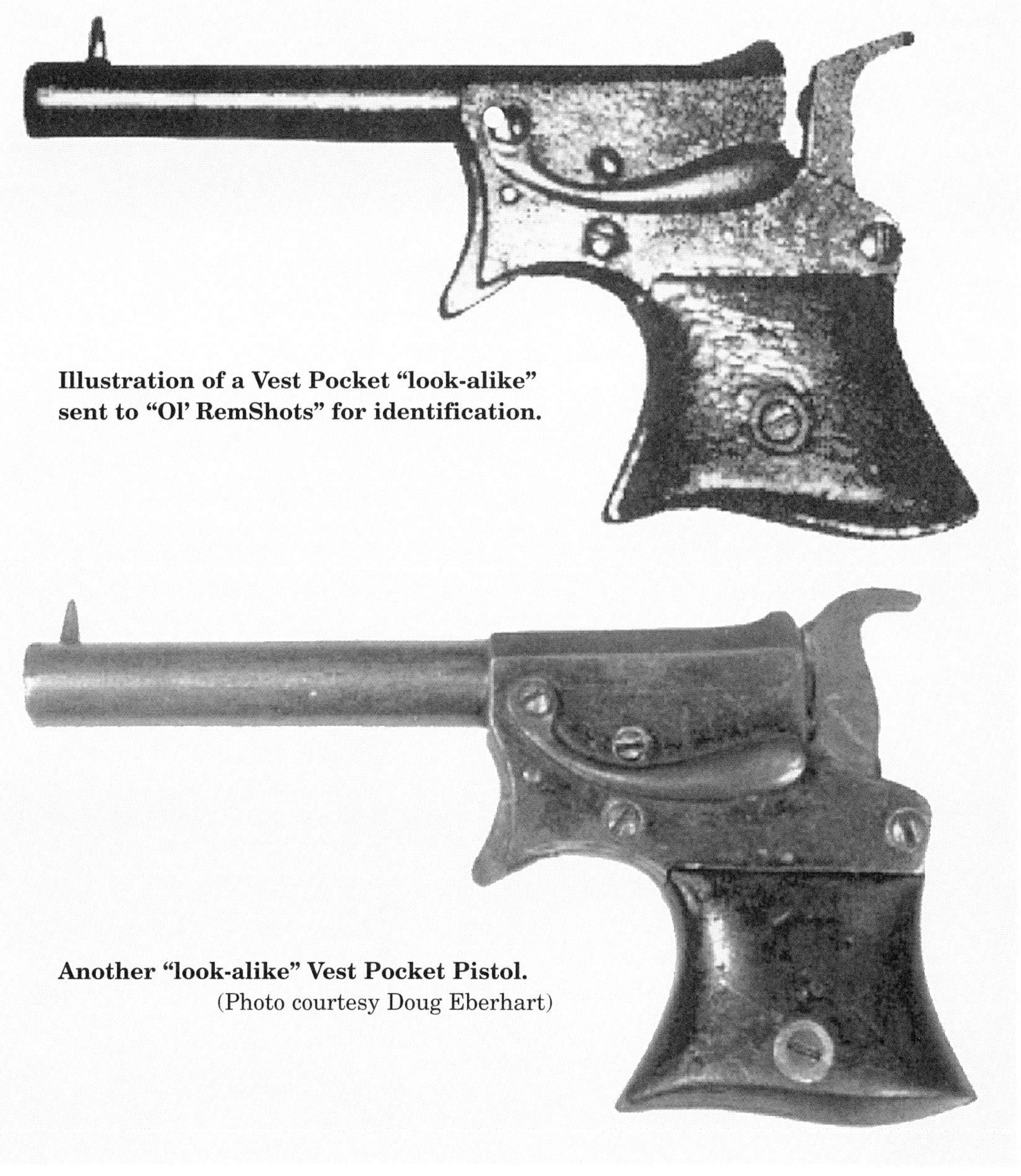

Illustration of a Vest Pocket "look-alike" sent to "Ol' RemShots" for identification.

Another "look-alike" Vest Pocket Pistol.
(Photo courtesy Doug Eberhart)

PRICE LIST

Of Rifle and Shot Gun Barrels, Pistols, Gun Canes, &c.

Cast Steel Barrels, of 6 lbs. wt. or less, each	$3 00
" " " over 6 lbs. extra pr lb.	40
Iron Barrels, 7 lbs. wt. or less, each	2 00
" " from 7 to 12 lbs., extra pr lb.	10
" " " 12 to 18 " " "	20
" " over 18 lbs., " "	40
Stubs Twisted, plain, usual proportions, each,	4 00
" " " over 6 lbs., extra pr lb.	40
" " fine, usual proportions, each	5 00
" " " over 6 lbs. wt. extra pr lb.	50
Matched Barrels, for Double Guns, Cast Steel, per pair,	6 50

Matched Barrels, Shot, for Double Guns, Cast Steel, price according to size.	
" " for doub. guns pl'n iron, pair	$4 00
" " stubs twisted plain, pr pair	8 00
" " " " fine, "	10 00
Rifling Barrels (gain twist) each	2 00
Fitting patent muzzle for target rifles, each	3 00
" Ball Starter " " " "	1 75
Rifle Telescopes with solid Steel Tubes, each	16 00
Cylinders for Rifling Machines, (smooth)	5 00
" " " " (rifled)	12 00
" with Index Wheel, Standards, Rods &c. fitted	25 00

HEAVY BARRELS, for Duck Guns, price according to size and form. CAST STEEL BARRELS, drilled from solid bar, with any required size and number of bores, and of any required exterior form, price according to size and form. For putting on Cone Seat, working to a guage, Grooving for rod and for Barrels of unusual proportions, an additional charge will be made. Also, an extra charge for *smaller calibre than* 150, and for Barrels *over* 3½ *feet long*.

Discount from the above prices, 5 per cent. on Bills of $50 *to* $100; 10 *pr cent. on Bills of* $100, *or upwards.*

Item	p'r doz.
BEAL'S Patent Revolver, Pocket size	$72 00
" " " Engraved, extra	3 00
" " " Second Size	96 00
" " " Engraved, extra	4 00
RIDER'S Pat. Rev'r Pocket size, self-cocking	75 00
" " Engraved, extra	3 00
" Parlor Pistol	15 00

Item	p'r doz.
Gun Cane, Rifle	$72 00
" " Rifle and Shot	108 00
Pistol Cases, (wood.)	9 00
Extra Cylinders, Pocket size	12 00
" " Engraved, extra	1 50
" " Second size	14 00
" " Engraved, extra	2 00

Percussion Caps for Pistols, metal-lined and water-proof, 85 cents per thousand.

We have now in process of manufacture a new and superior CARTRIDGE LOADING REVOLVER which will be ready for market in the course of two or three months. We are also preparing to manufacture BEAL'S NAVY SIZE REVOLVER, (7½ barrel, carrying 50 balls to the pound,) which will be in market next Spring.

CORRESPONDENTS, ordering Barrels, will greatly oblige us by observing, as far as possible, the following rules:—All orders should be *plainly written out in a* LIST, which will prevent mistakes in transferring to our order book.

All the Dimensions of barrels—LENGTH, BORE and WEIGHT, (or diameter,) should be given in *figures*, and no reference made to previous orders, if possible.

In ordering, mention, 1st, Number of Barrels; 2d, Material; 3d, Length; 4th, Bore; 5th, Weight or diameter; 6th, other particulars, if any.

☞ Directions for forwarding should accompany *each* order, mentioning whether to forward by Rail Road, as freight, or by Express.

E. REMINGTON & SONS.

Ilion, Herkimer Co., N. Y., October, 1860.

The basic goal of this research was to determine Remington Vest Pocket Pistol specifications, the calibers in which they were produced, the quantities made, and the materials and finishes used, as well as to develop component parts lists and provide exploded views of each pistol.

Seven specific questions need to be addressed. These interrogatives serve as the chapter titles you are about to encounter:

1. What shall we call them?
2. What's the serial number story?
3. How many were manufactured?
4. What calibers were produced?
5. During what period of time were they made?
6. What were their specifications?
7. Did Remington build Vest Pocket Buggy Rifles?

Chapter One

What Shall We Call Them?

In the September 1997 monograph, the Remington Vest Pocket Pistols were referred to as Remington's Vest Pocket Pistol and the Celebrated Saw-Handle-Grip Pocket Pistol." Some previous publications, as well as some more recent ones, have chosen to call them "The .22 cal. Vest Pocket Pistol" and the "Split Breech Vest Pocket Pistol."

There are publications that refer to these small handguns as:
"Remington Vest Pockets"
"Remington Saw Grip Pistols"
"Saw Handle Deringers"
"Elliot's Single Shot Derringer"
"Remington Vest Pocket Pistols"
"Vest Pocket Derringers"
...among other things.

Robert W.D. Ball listed them as "Remington Vest Pocket Pistols" and "Remington Split Breech Derringers" (a.k.a. "Saw Handle Deringer"). Doug Eberhart referred to the larger caliber models as "Split Breech Deringers." Alden Hatch refers to them as "Vest Pocket Pistols." K.D. Kirkland calls them "Remington Vest Pocket Pistols, (a.k.a. "Saw Handle Derringers"). Schwing/Houze used the labels "Vest Pocket Pistols" for the .22 caliber models and "Large-Bore Vest Pocket Pistols" for the No. 2 and No. 3 Sizes, in the *Standard Catalog of Firearms.*

The Collecting of Guns, edited by James L. Serven (1964), states that Remington Vest Pocket Pistols were manufactured in .22 caliber, .30 caliber and .41 caliber. It also contends that a few of the "Split-breech Pistols" breech-loaders were fitted with skeleton stocks and are referred to by collectors as "Buggy Rifles."

Leon Wier, in *RSA Journal* articles, revealed that today's collectors refer to them (No. 1 Size) as .22 Vest Pockets. He pointed out that the Remington Vest Pocket Pistols have been referred to as Vest Pocket Pistols, Derringers and just Vest Pockets. Flayderman used similar terminology with "No. 1, No. 2 and No. 3 Sizes," explaining them as Remington labels. Another source, Harold L. Peterson's *The Remington Historical Treasury of American Guns* (1966) states that Remington called these easily concealed weapons "Vest Pocket Pistols." The Antique Firearm Network on the Internet provides the designations "Remington Vest Pocket Pistol" and "Remington Split Breech Derringer."

So, What *Did* Remington Call Them?

A Remington advertisement of the 1860s (see below) describes an illustration of a "split-breech" model as simply a "Single Barrel Pistol," New Pattern – Two Sizes, with swinging breech, Nos. 32 and 41.

As seen on the facing page, Remington did, in fact, refer to these pistols as "Vest Pocket Pistols" No. 1, No. 2 and No. 3 Sizes in their 1870 catalog. No. 1 and No. 3 sizes are illustrated.

Again, in a reprint of page 34 (shown on page 58) from Remington's 1877 catalog entitled: "Illustrated REMINGTONS' BREECH-LOADING Rifles, Shot Guns, Revolvers, Repeaters and Ammunition, ca.1877" they used the reference "Remingtons' Vest Pocket Pistol."

Some sources have added the term "Split-Breech" in reference to the larger caliber model Vest Pocket Pistols. As illustrated on page 20, Remington used "Celebrated SAW-HANDLE-GRIP Pocket Pistol" to identify their Split-Breech models. Remington added that these pistols were "finely made and were easy working." They emphasized a "Stirrup Look." The most common term of reference is simply **Remington Vest Pocket Pistol.** Let's use that to agree on just what they should be called.

The designation "Remington Vest Pocket Pistol" (incorporated in the titles of the '97 monograph and this book) is hereby nominated. To keep it simple in this text, they will all be referred to as "Remington Vest Pocket Pistols."

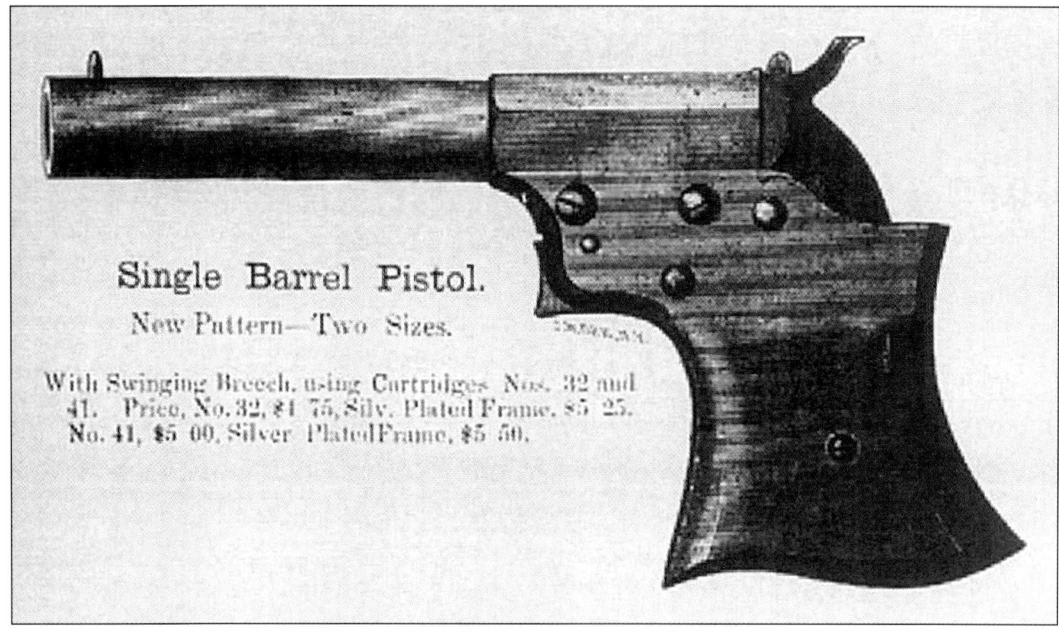

Remington & Sons advertisement, ca.1860.

(Facing page) This page from Remington's 1870 catalog reproduced in actual size to reflect the exact size of the .22 caliber rimfire short Vest Pocket Pistol and the .41 caliber rimfire short, split-breech Vest Pocket Pistol.

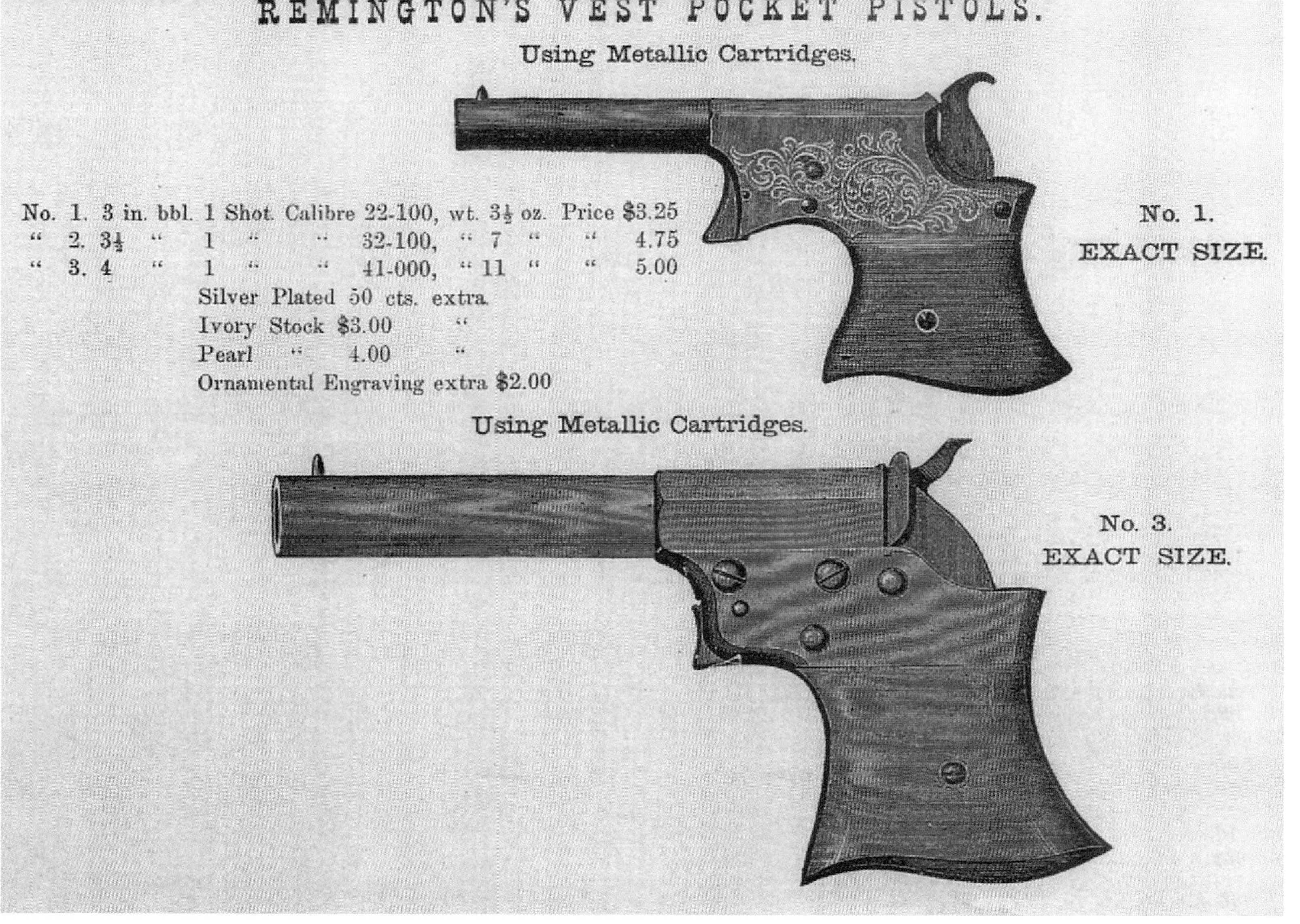
REMINGTON'S VEST POCKET PISTOLS.
Using Metallic Cartridges.
No. 1. 3 in. bbl. 1 Shot. Calibre 22-100, wt. 3½ oz. Price $3.25
" 2. 3½ " 1 " " 32-100, " 7 " " 4.75
" 3. 4 " 1 " " 41-000, " 11 " " 5.00
Silver Plated 50 cts. extra.
Ivory Stock $3.00 "
Pearl " 4.00 "
Ornamental Engraving extra $2.00
No. 1.
EXACT SIZE.
Using Metallic Cartridges.
No. 3.
EXACT SIZE.

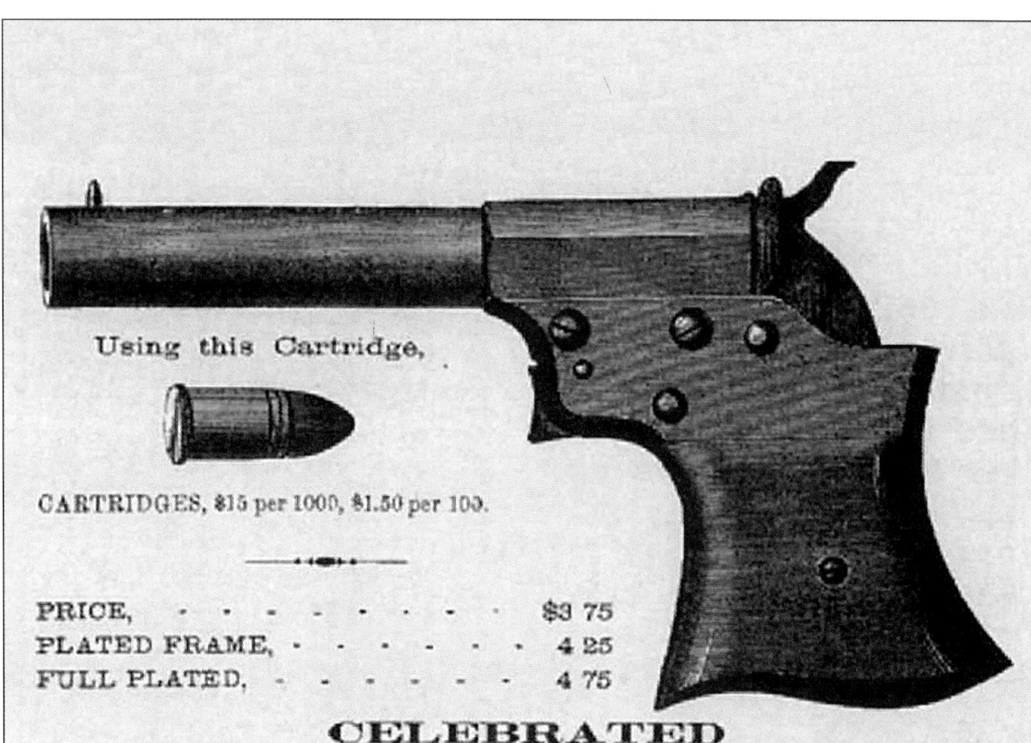

CELEBRATED

SAW-HANDLE-GRIP POCKET PISTOL,

Remington Breech-Loader, Shooting Deringer Ball,

THIS PISTOL IS THE

Cheapest and Best Single Shot in the Market,

Giving a Firm Grip against Recoil, and having a Finely Made and Easy Working

"STIRRUP LOCK."

MANUFACTURED BY

ARMORY, E. REMINGTON & SONS,

ILION, 281 & 283 BROADWAY,

Remington & Sons advertisement, ca.1860.

Remington, No. 1 Size, .22 caliber rimfire short, Vest Pocket Pistol, SN12005, blue finish, engraved, rosewood grips.
(Elliott Burka Photo)

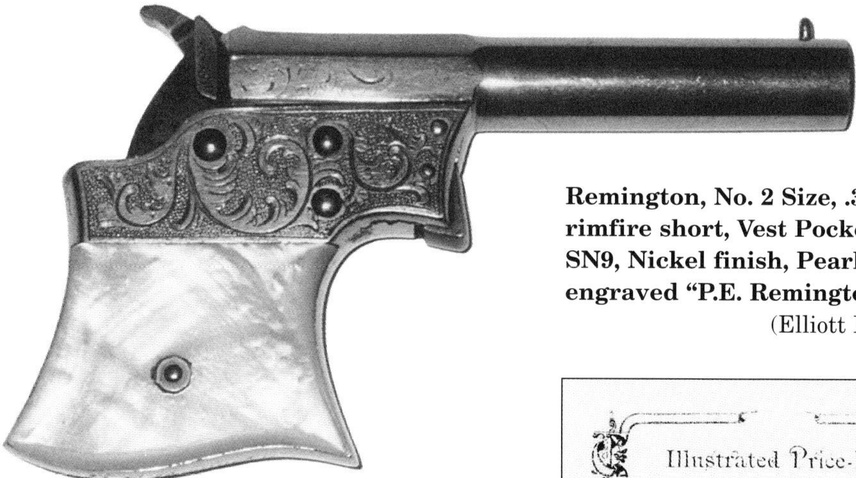

Remington, No. 2 Size, .30 caliber, rimfire short, Vest Pocket Pistol, SN9, Nickel finish, Pearl grips, engraved "P.E. Remington".
(Elliott Burka Photo)

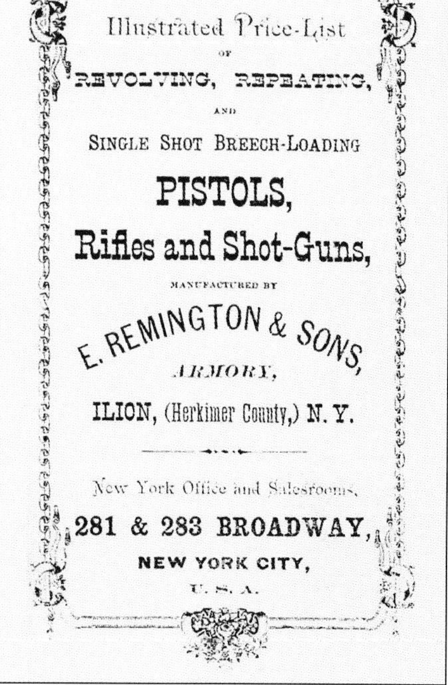

Illustrated Price-List
OF
REVOLVING, REPEATING,
AND
SINGLE SHOT BREECH-LOADING
PISTOLS,
Rifles and Shot-Guns,
MANUFACTURED BY
E. REMINGTON & SONS,
ARMORY,
ILION, (Herkimer County,) N. Y.
New York Office and Salesrooms,
281 & 283 BROADWAY,
NEW YORK CITY,
U. S. A.

Pictured here and on page 22 are the four Vest Pocket Pistols: .22 caliber, .30 caliber, .32 caliber and .41 caliber.

Sometime after the Civil War, Remington issued an illustrated price list consisting of ten panels on each side of a sheet of paper. When folded to expose one panel at a time, this piece formed a pocket-sized catalog of Remington products that were available at that time.

The impressively bordered title page is shown at right, while two actual pages from the catalog are shown on pages 23 and 24.

(The shaded edges and the imperfect printing reproduction of these price lists reflect their age and the results of the "transparent tape" used to hold them together.)

Remington, No. 2 Size, .32 caliber, rimfire short, Vest Pocket Pistol, SN191, factory engraved, in the white, walnut grips.
(Author's Collection)

Remington, No. 3 Size, .41 caliber, rimfire short, Vest Pocket Pistol, SN1310, silver finish, walnut grips, acid-etched engraving.
(Elliott Burka Photo)

Eighteen Remington products were advertised in this price list. (Twenty if you count the two illustrated cane guns.) Association with other Remington products that were available during the same period in which Vest Pockets were being manufactured should shed some light on the general time frame during which Remington produced Vest Pocket Pistols.

Remington's .22 caliber Vest Pocket Pistol and the .41 caliber Saw-Handle-Grip Vest Pocket Pistol occupied two panels in the price list. Though the reproduction quality is a long way from perfect, these enlarged panels reveal an aspect of Remington's advertising between 1863 and 1880.

The panel at the top of page 25 appeared in both product price lists being discussed. The panel at the bottom of page 25 appeared only in the first of these two published price lists. This indicates that production of the .22 caliber Remington Vest Pocket Pistols was still underway after the larger No. 2 and No. 3 Size Vest Pocket Pistols were discontinued.

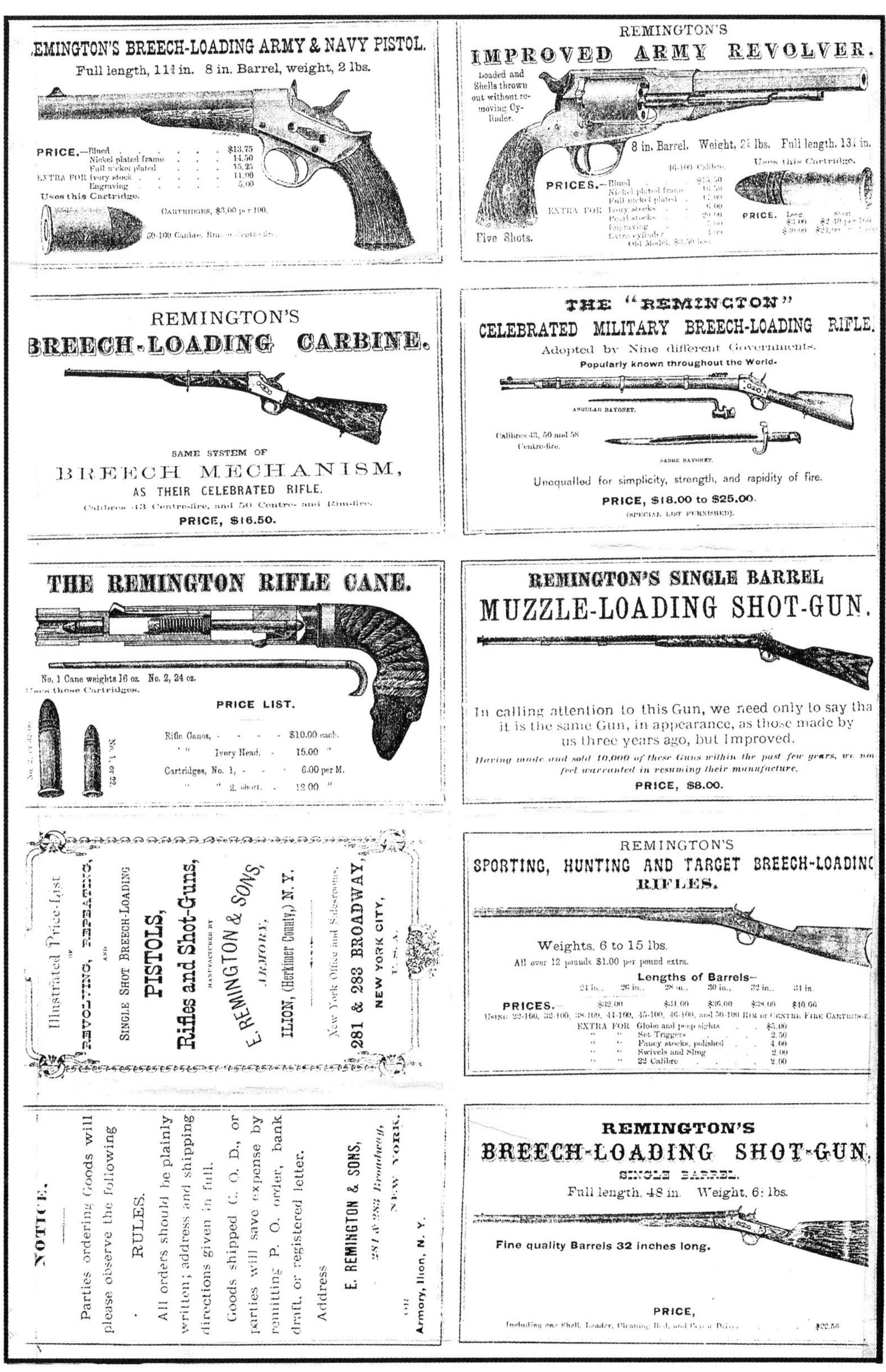
EMINGTON'S BREECH-LOADING ARMY & NAVY PISTOL.
Full length, 11½ in. 8 in. Barrel, weight, 2 lbs.
PRICE.—Blued $13.75
Nickel plated frame 14.50
Full nickel plated 15.25
EXTRA FOR Ivory stock 11.00
Engraving 5.00
Uses this Cartridge.
REMINGTON'S
IMPROVED ARMY REVOLVER.
Loaded and Shells thrown out without removing Cylinder.
8 in. Barrel. Weight, 2½ lbs. Full length, 13½ in.
Uses this Cartridge.
PRICES.—
PRICE.
Five Shots.
REMINGTON'S
BREECH-LOADING CARBINE.
SAME SYSTEM OF
BREECH MECHANISM,
AS THEIR CELEBRATED RIFLE.
PRICE, $16.50.
THE "REMINGTON"
CELEBRATED MILITARY BREECH-LOADING RIFLE.
Adopted by Nine different Governments.
Popularly known throughout the World.
ANGULAR BAYONET.
SABRE BAYONET.
Unequalled for simplicity, strength, and rapidity of fire.
PRICE, $18.00 to $25.00.
THE REMINGTON RIFLE CANE.
No. 1 Cane weights 16 oz. No. 2, 24 oz.
Uses these Cartridges.
PRICE LIST.
Rifle Canes, - - - - $10.00 each.
" " Ivory Head, - 15.00 "
Cartridges, No. 1, - - - 6.00 per M.
" " 2, short, - 12.00 "
REMINGTON'S SINGLE BARREL
MUZZLE-LOADING SHOT-GUN.
In calling attention to this Gun, we need only to say tha it is the same Gun, in appearance, as those made by us three years ago, but Improved.
PRICE, $8.00.
Illustrated Price-List of
REVOLVING, REPEATING, and
SINGLE SHOT BREECH-LOADING
PISTOLS,
Rifles and Shot-Guns,
MANUFACTURED BY
E. REMINGTON & SONS,
ARMORY,
ILION, (Herkimer County,) N. Y.
New York Office and Salesrooms,
281 & 283 BROADWAY,
NEW YORK CITY,
U. S. A.
REMINGTON'S
SPORTING, HUNTING AND TARGET BREECH-LOADINC RIFLES.
Weights. 6 to 15 lbs.
All over 12 pounds $1.00 per pound extra.
Lengths of Barrels—
PRICES.
NOTICE.
Parties ordering Goods will please observe the following
RULES.
All orders should be plainly written; address and shipping directions given in full.
Goods shipped C. O. D., or parties will save expense by remitting P. O. order, bank draft, or registered letter.
Address
E. REMINGTON & SONS,
281 & 283 Broadway,
NEW YORK.
OR
Armory, Ilion, N. Y.
REMINGTON'S
BREECH-LOADING SHOT-GUN,
SINGLE BARREL.
Full length. 48 in. Weight. 6½ lbs.
Fine quality Barrels 32 inches long.
PRICE,

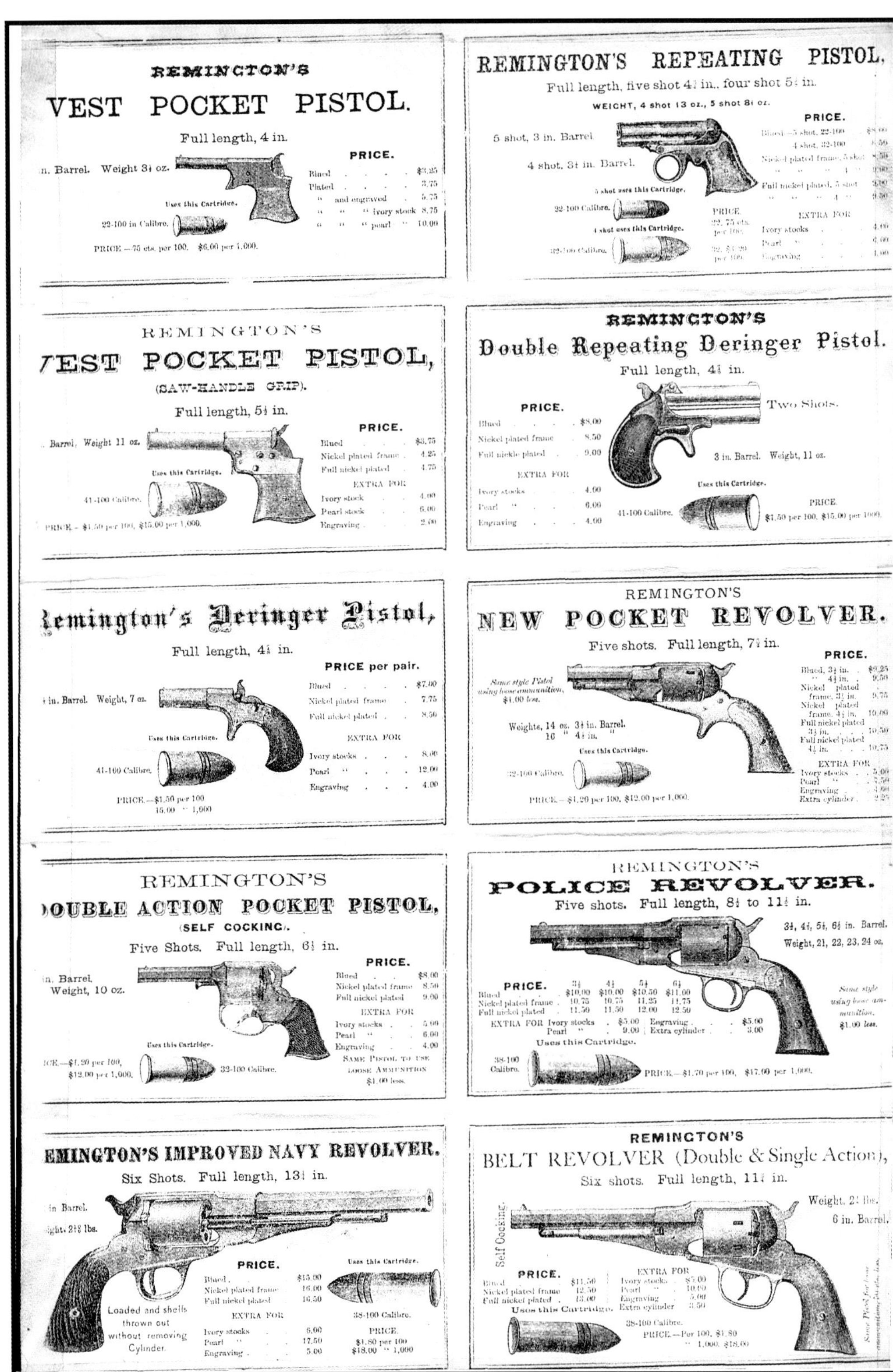
REMINGTON'S
VEST POCKET PISTOL.
Full length, 4 in.
n. Barrel. Weight 3½ oz.
PRICE.
Blued $3.25
Plated 3.75
" and engraved . 5.75
" " " ivory stock 8.75
" " " pearl " 10.00
Uses this Cartridge.
22-100 in Calibre.
PRICE.—75 cts. per 100. $6.00 per 1,000.
REMINGTON'S REPEATING PISTOL,
Full length, five shot 4½ in., four shot 5½ in.
WEIGHT, 4 shot 13 oz., 5 shot 8½ oz.
5 shot, 3 in. Barrel
4 shot, 3½ in. Barrel.
PRICE.
5 shot uses this Cartridge.
22-100 Calibre.
4 shot uses this Cartridge.
EXTRA FOR
Ivory stocks
Pearl "
Engraving
REMINGTON'S
VEST POCKET PISTOL,
(SAW-HANDLE GRIP).
Full length, 5½ in.
Barrel, Weight 11 oz.
PRICE.
Blued . . . $3.75
Nickel plated frame . 4.25
Full nickel plated . 4.75
EXTRA FOR
Ivory stock . . 4.00
Pearl stock . . 6.00
Engraving . . 2.00
Uses this Cartridge.
41-100 Calibre.
PRICE.—$1.50 per 100, $15.00 per 1,000.
REMINGTON'S
Double Repeating Deringer Pistol.
Full length, 4¾ in.
Two Shots.
PRICE.
Blued . . . $8.00
Nickel plated frame . 8.50
Full nickle plated . 9.00
EXTRA FOR
Ivory stocks . . 4.00
Pearl " . . 6.00
Engraving . . . 4.00
3 in. Barrel. Weight, 11 oz.
Uses this Cartridge.
41-100 Calibre.
PRICE.
$1.50 per 100, $15.00 per 1000.
Remington's Deringer Pistol,
Full length, 4½ in.
in. Barrel. Weight, 7 oz.
PRICE per pair.
Blued $7.00
Nickel plated frame . 7.75
Full nickel plated . 8.50
EXTRA FOR
Ivory stocks . . . 8.00
Pearl " . . . 12.00
Engraving . . . 4.00
Uses this Cartridge.
41-100 Calibre.
PRICE.—$1.50 per 100
15.00 " 1,000
REMINGTON'S
NEW POCKET REVOLVER.
Five shots. Full length, 7½ in.
Same style Pistol using loose ammunition, $1.00 less.
Weights, 14 oz. 3½ in. Barrel.
16 " 4½ in. "
Uses this Cartridge.
32-100 Calibre.
PRICE.—$1.20 per 100, $12.00 per 1,000.
PRICE.
Blued, 3½ in. . $9.25
" 4½ in. . 9.50
Nickel plated frame, 3½ in. 9.75
Nickel plated frame, 4½ in. 10.00
Full nickel plated 3½ in. . . 10.50
Full nickel plated 4½ in. . . 10.75
EXTRA FOR
Ivory stocks . . 5.00
Pearl " . . 7.50
Engraving . . 4.00
Extra cylinder . . 2.25
REMINGTON'S
DOUBLE ACTION POCKET PISTOL,
(SELF COCKING).
Five Shots. Full length, 6½ in.
in. Barrel.
Weight, 10 oz.
PRICE.
Blued . . $8.00
Nickel plated frame 8.50
Full nickel plated 9.00
EXTRA FOR
Ivory stocks . . 5.00
Pearl " . . 6.00
Engraving . . 4.00
SAME PISTOL TO USE LOOSE AMMUNITION $1.00 less.
Uses this Cartridge.
PRICE.—$1.20 per 100, $12.00 per 1,000.
32-100 Calibre.
REMINGTON'S
POLICE REVOLVER.
Five shots. Full length, 8½ to 11½ in.
3½, 4½, 5½, 6½ in. Barrel.
Weight, 21, 22, 23, 24 oz.
PRICE. 3½ 4½ 5½ 6½
Blued . . $10.00 $10.00 $10.50 $11.00
Nickel plated frame . 10.75 10.75 11.25 11.75
Full nickel plated . 11.50 11.50 12.00 12.50
EXTRA FOR Ivory stocks . $5.00 | Engraving . . $5.00
Pearl " . 9.00 | Extra cylinder . . 3.00
Same style using loose ammunition, $1.00 less.
Uses this Cartridge.
38-100 Calibre.
PRICE.—$1.70 per 100, $17.00 per 1,000.
REMINGTON'S IMPROVED NAVY REVOLVER.
Six Shots. Full length, 13½ in.
in Barrel.
Weight, 2½ lbs.
PRICE.
Blued . . $15.00
Nickel plated frame 16.00
Full nickel plated 16.50
EXTRA FOR
Ivory stocks . . 6.00
Pearl " . . 17.50
Engraving . . 5.00
Uses this Cartridge.
38-100 Calibre.
PRICE.
$1.80 per 100
$18.00 " 1,000
Loaded and shells thrown out without removing Cylinder.
REMINGTON'S
BELT REVOLVER (Double & Single Action),
Six shots. Full length, 11½ in.
Weight, 2½ lbs.
6 in. Barrel.
Self Cocking.
PRICE.
Blued . . $11.50
Nickel plated frame 12.50
Full nickel plated . 13.00
EXTRA FOR
Ivory stocks . $5.00
Pearl " . 10.00
Engraving . 5.00
Extra cylinder 3.50
Uses this Cartridge.
38-100 Calibre.
PRICE.—Per 100, $1.80
" 1,000, $18.00

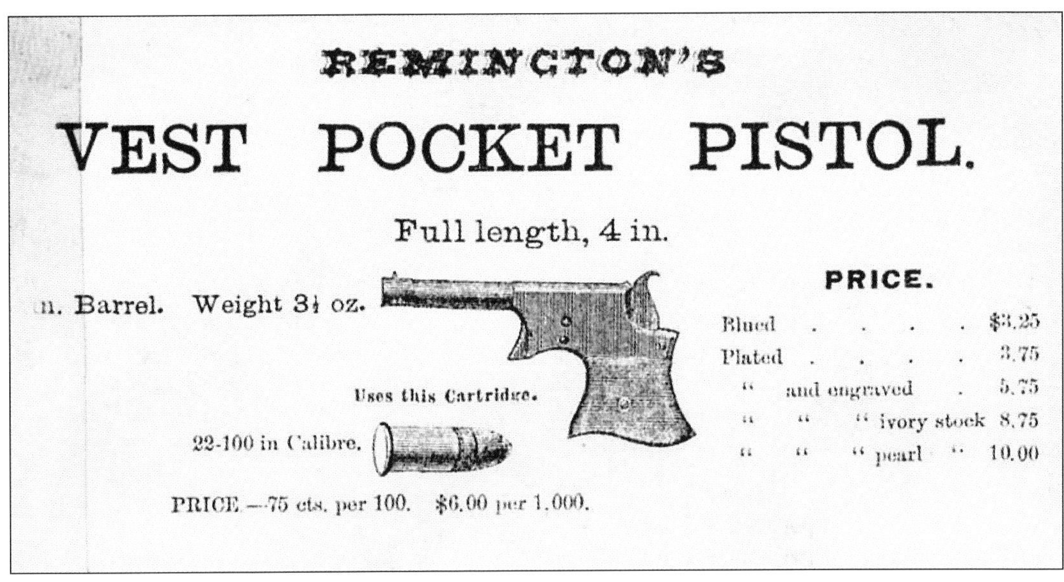

Two panels advertising .22 caliber Vest Pocket Pistol (above) **and .41 caliber** (below) **from a folding pocket-sized Remington price list.**

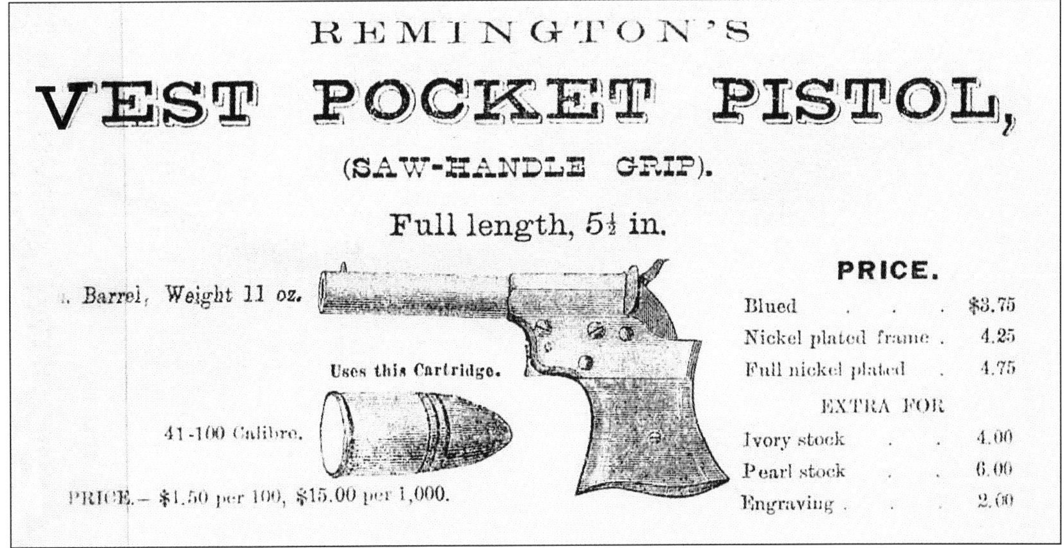

Other Remington products illustrated in the handy multi-fold advertisement piece were:

- The "Deringer" Single Shot Pistol with bird's-head grip, in .41 caliber.
- Remington's Double Action Pocket Pistol, .32 caliber with a two-piece cylinder.
- The improved Navy Revolver, .38 caliber.
- Double Repeating Deringer Pistol, over/under .41 caliber.
- Remington's New Model Pocket Revolver, .32 caliber, with two-piece cylinder.
- The Police Revolver .38 caliber, with two-piece cylinder.
- Remington's Repeating 4-shot and 5-shot repeating pistols
- Remington's Single Barrel Muzzleloading Shot-gun.

- Remington's Belt Revolver (Double and Single Action), .38 caliber with two-piece cylinder.
- Breech-Loading Army and Navy Pistol (a Rolling Block pistol), .50 caliber rim or centerfire.
- Breech-Loading Carbine (Rolling Block) in .43 centerfire and .50 caliber center and rimfire.
- The Remington Rifle Cane. No. 1 in .22 caliber and the No. 2 in .32 caliber.
- Remington's Improved Army Revolver, .46 caliber with two-piece cylinder.
- The Celebrated Military Breech-Loading Rifle (Rolling Block), .43 caliber and .50 caliber rimfire and .50 caliber centerfire.
- Remington's Single Barrel Breech-Loading Shot-gun.
- Sporting, Hunting and Target Breech-Loading (Rolling Block) Rifles in several calibers (.22 caliber up to .50 caliber).

Sometime later, Remington put out another folding illustrated price list. The title panel of this publication (pictured below, left) was very similar to the previously mentioned list. A noticeable difference was the addition of fine print identifying the printer, Citizen Print, Ilion, NY.

The .41 (41-100) caliber Saw-Handle-Grip Vest Pocket Pistol was missing from the latter rendition. The .22 caliber was included, using the same advertising copy as in the previous list. There were six panels on each side of this illustrated price list, twelve panels in all.

In addition to the Vest Pocket .22, the Rider's Patent Magazine Pistol in ".32 calibre" and Remington's No. 1 Revolver (Smoot's Patent) in .30 cal. were included. (Please take note that these two new additions were listed as .32 calibre and .30 cal., respectively).

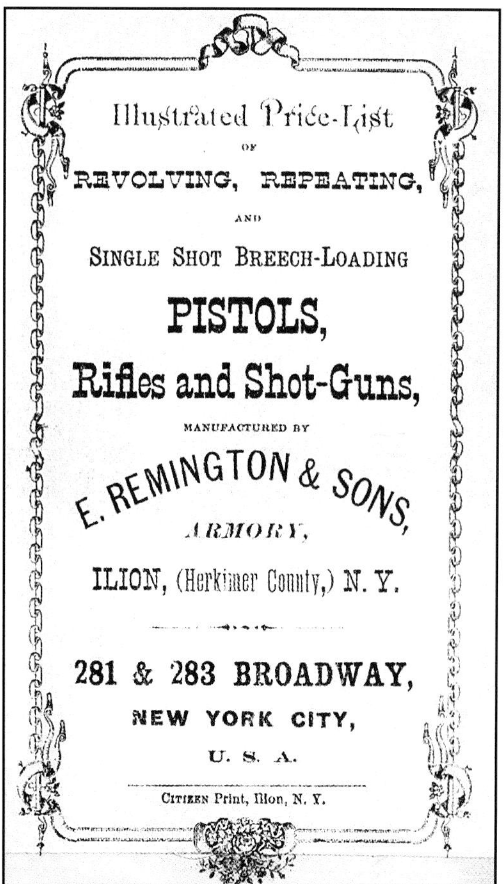

Illustrated Price-List
OF
REVOLVING, REPEATING,
AND
SINGLE SHOT BREECH-LOADING
PISTOLS,
Rifles and Shot-Guns,
MANUFACTURED BY
E. REMINGTON & SONS,
ARMORY,
ILION, (Herkimer County,) N. Y.

281 & 283 BROADWAY,
NEW YORK CITY,
U. S. A.

CITIZEN Print, Ilion, N. Y.

NOTICE.

Parties ordering Goods will please observe the following

RULES.

All orders should be plainly written; address and shipping directions given in full.

Goods shipped C. O. D., or parties will save expense by remitting P. O. order, bank draft, or registered letter.

Address

E. REMINGTON & SONS,
281 & 283 Broadway,
NEW YORK.
OR
Armory, Ilion, N. Y.

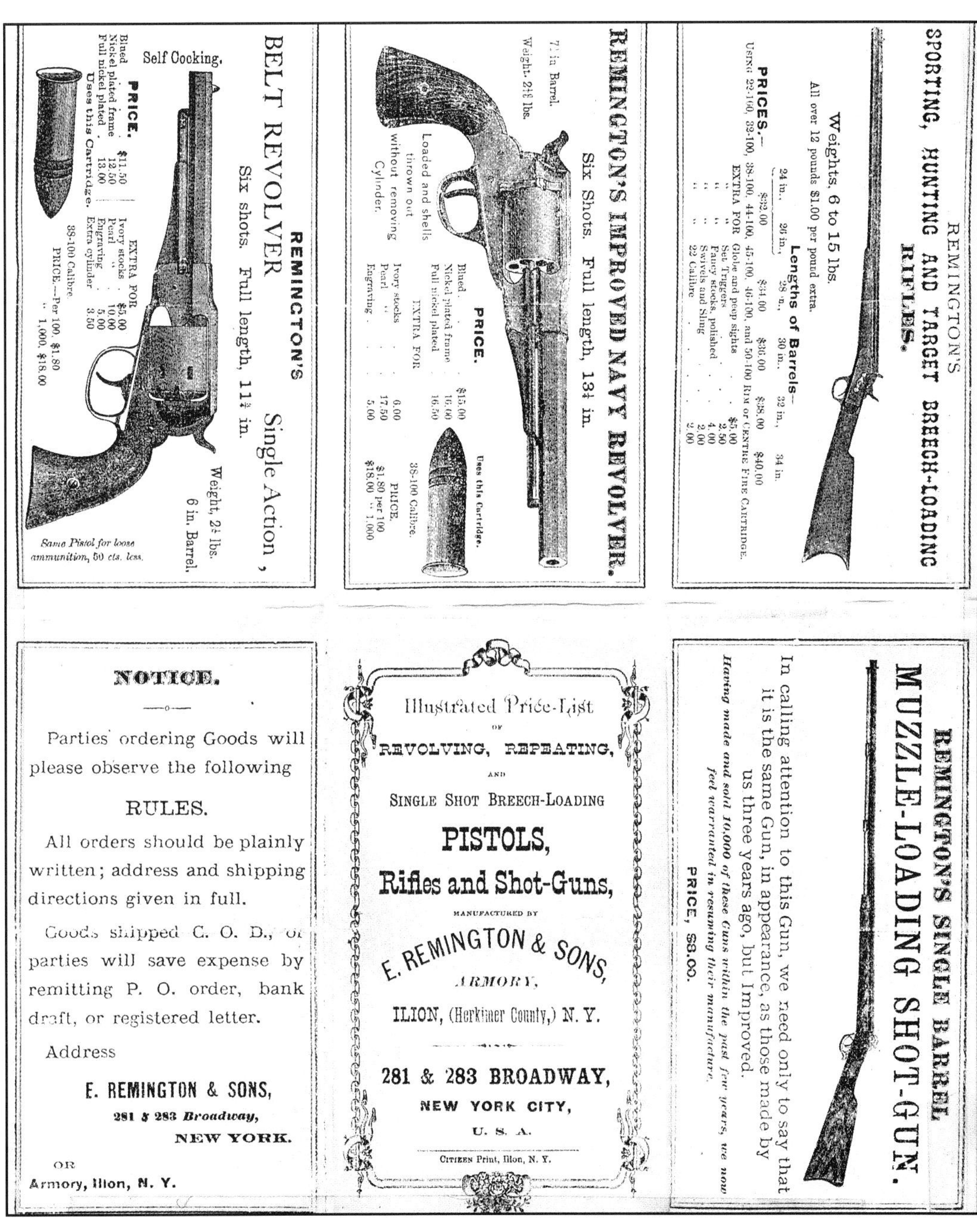

REMINGTON'S
SPORTING, HUNTING AND TARGET BREECH-LOADING RIFLES.

Weights, 6 to 15 lbs.
All over 12 pounds $1.00 per pound extra.

Lengths of Barrels—

	24 in.,	26 in.,	28 in.,	30 in.,	32 in.,	34 in.
PRICES.—	$32.00		$34.00	$36.00	$38.00	$40.00

Using 22-100, 32-100, 38-100, 44-100, 45-100, 46-100, and 50-100 Rim or Centre Fire Cartridge.

EXTRA FOR	
Globe and peep sights	$5.00
Set Triggers	2.50
Fancy stocks, polished	4.00
Swivels and Sling	2.00
22 Calibre	2.00

REMINGTON'S IMPROVED NAVY REVOLVER.

Six Shots. Full length, 13¼ in.
7½ in Barrel.
Weight 2¼ lbs.

Loaded and shells thrown out without removing Cylinder.

PRICE.

Blued	$15.00
Nickel plated frame	16.00
Full nickel plated	16.50
EXTRA FOR	
Ivory stocks	6.00
Pearl	17.50
Engraving	5.00

Uses this Cartridge.
38-100 Calibre.
PRICE,
$1.80 per 100.
$18.00 " 1,000

REMINGTON'S
BELT REVOLVER
Single Action,
Six shots. Full length, 11¾ in.
Weight, 2¼ lbs.
6 in. Barrel.

Self Cocking.

PRICE.

		EXTRA FOR	
Blued	$11.50	Ivory stocks	$5.00
Nickel plated frame	12.50	Pearl	10.00
Full nickel plated	13.00	Engraving	5.00
		Extra cylinder	3.50

Uses this Cartridge.
38-100 Calibre
PRICE.—Per 100, $1.80
" 1,000, $18.00

Same Pistol for loose ammunition, 50 cts. less.

NOTICE.

Parties ordering Goods will please observe the following

RULES.

All orders should be plainly written; address and shipping directions given in full.

Goods shipped C. O. D., or parties will save expense by remitting P. O. order, bank draft, or registered letter.

Address

E. REMINGTON & SONS,
281 & 283 Broadway,
NEW YORK.

OR

Armory, Ilion, N. Y.

Illustrated Price-List
OF
REVOLVING, REPEATING,
AND
SINGLE SHOT BREECH-LOADING
PISTOLS,
Rifles and Shot-Guns,
MANUFACTURED BY
E. REMINGTON & SONS,
ARMORY,
ILION, (Herkimer County,) N. Y.

281 & 283 BROADWAY,
NEW YORK CITY,
U. S. A.

CITIZEN Print, Ilion, N. Y.

REMINGTON'S SINGLE BARREL
MUZZLE-LOADING SHOT-GUN.

In calling attention to this Gun, we need only to say that it is the same Gun, in appearance, as those made by us three years ago, but Improved.

Having made and sold 10,000 of these Guns within the past few years, we now feel warranted in resuming their manufacture.

PRICE, $8.00.

The products carried over from the previous price list were still identified using caliber designations of 22-100, 32-100, 38-100, 44-100, 45-100 and 50-100 rim, and in the case of some, centerfire cartridge. Still offered were the Remington New Pocket Revolver, the Police Revolver, the Improved Navy Revolver (which could be loaded and the shells thrown out without removing the cylinder), the Belt Revolver, Sporting, Hunting and Target Breech-Loading Rifles plus the Single Barrel Muzzle-Loading Shotgun.

Both of the referenced price lists featured the Armory in Ilion (Herkimer County), N.Y., as well as the New York Office and Salesrooms at 281 & 283 Broadway, New York City, U.S.A. address.

Remington included a "Rules for Purchasing a Remington Product" panel in each of the price lists. Both of the folding pocket-sized price lists included a panel devoted to a "Notice" to "Parties Ordering Goods."

The common-sense rules (shown enlarged on page 26) were directions soliciting plainly written orders requesting that address and shipping directions be provided in full. There were instructions for C.O.D. deliveries and remittance information that simply told potential buyers that a P.O. (money) order, a bank draft or registered letter could save expense.

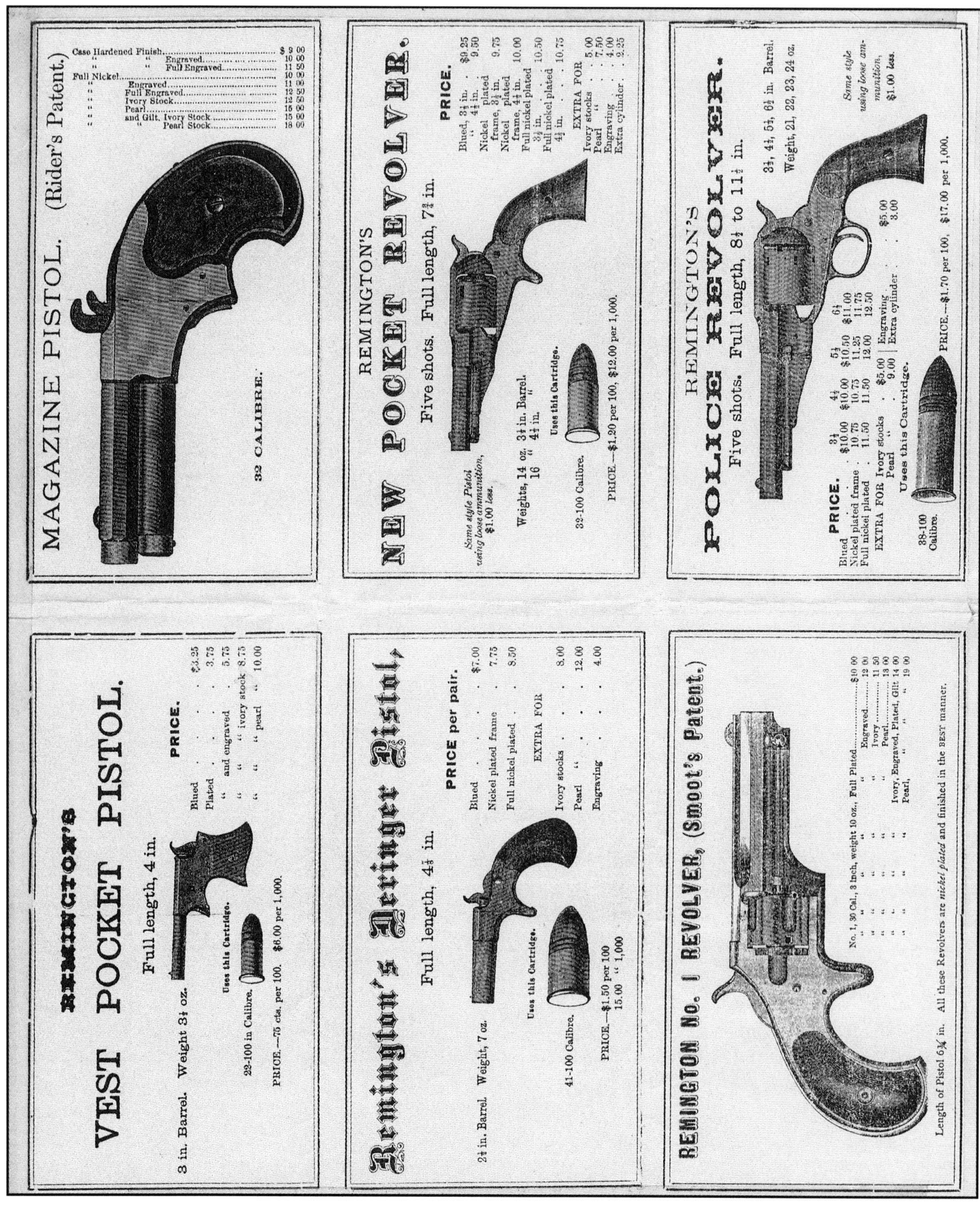

Chapter Two

What's the Serial Number Story?

"Remington used a single consecutive series of serial numbers for their Vest Pocket Pistols for all of the four calibers they produced!"

Initially, it appeared quite probable that each caliber of Remington Vest Pocket Pistol had a unique series of sequential serial numbers, with each series starting at Number 1. That assumption was based on the numerous responses to the requests on the research/survey forms distributed through the generosity of the *RSA Journal*. This was early in the research process, when the research forms, cards, letters, and phone calls were just beginning to be received. Very few duplicate serial numbers were reported.

Responses to the survey included suggestions as to how to improve the questionnaire. With these suggestions integrated, a second distribution of research forms was made. Efforts to find additional weapons to scrutinize in current publications, in museums, at auctions and/or in auction catalogs, on the internet and at gun shows, were intensified. As the volume of responses to the survey increased, the frequency of duplicate serial numbers failed to increase.

In May 1977, Jim Shaffer of Irwin, Pennsylvania, presented the serial number search with a terrific boost. He had been collecting and logging Remington Vest Pocket serial numbers for more than 30 years. During that period of time, Jim had accumulated 127 Vest Pocket serial numbers. Though many of the serial numbers Jim provided were already included in the survey, his contributions were significant.

The number of specimens, by caliber and the lowest-to-highest serial number, which he reported were:

Caliber	Serial # Range	No. of Specimens
.22	3–16824	65
.30 (No minimum # provided)	–7688	18 (7 brass frames)
.32	191–3515	12
.41	13–4812	32
	Total	127

When the initial booklet was published (Sept. 1997), the survey's serial number base had grown to 191 different Vest Pocket Pistol serial numbers. By August 31, 1999, when input was initially closed, a total of 335 Remington Vest Pocket Pistol serial numbers (all calibers) had been logged. As additional serial numbers were acquired in September 1999, that quantity grew to 344, when input was actually halted at the end of November.

By February 10, 2000, more serial numbers were added, bringing the total to 362. Even with the larger sample of serial numbers, duplicate serial numbers still did not appear.

Let's look at the sequence of serial numbers submitted, and to which calibers they were assigned:

- Serial number 1 was reported found on a Remington .22 caliber rimfire short, No. 1 Size, Vest Pocket Pistol.
- Serial number 2 was given to a Remington .30 caliber rimfire short, No. 2 Size, Vest Pocket Pistol.
- Serial number 3 was also a .30 caliber Vest Pocket Pistol.
- Serial numbers 4 and 5 have not surfaced. Serial number 6 has been reported as a .22 cal.
- Serial numbers 7, 8, 9 and 11 were .30 caliber (Serial number 10 and serial number 12 have not been reported).
- The lowest serial number reported on a Remington .41 caliber rimfire short, No. 3 Size Vest Pocket Pistol was 13.
- The lowest serial number on a Remington .32 caliber rimfire short, No. 2 size, Remington Vest Pocket Pistol submitted was 40.
- Serial number 32 was reported in both .30 caliber and .41 caliber. (The submission in .41 caliber was from an offer sell-dated more than 30 years ago, which was sent in by one of the respondents to the survey and not verifiable.)
- Serial number 81 showed up twice. Once on a .22 caliber, No. 1 Size and again on a .41 caliber, No. 3 Size. Interestingly, the serial number on the .22 caliber Vest Pocket Pistol is on the frame, while a different serial number (1935) appears on the underside of the barrel. The report on the .41 caliber model reveals that the serial number on the frame is also #81, and a different number (#2183) is on the underside of the barrel.
- Serial #349 was reported as being seen in two different editions of *The Gun Report*. (In the Oct. 1970 issue, pg. 3, as a .32 cal., and in the Feb. 1977 issue, pg. 3, as a .22 cal.)

The referenced magazines were sought to determine if, in fact, these duplicate serial numbers did really exist. Fortunately, both of the issues were still available from the publisher. Unfortunately, review of both issues has proved nothing tangible. There were advertisements in both issues, and both ads were for the same Nevada gun dealer.

The 1970 ad reads:

> *No. 1483 - REMINGTON VEST POCKET .32 DERRINGER. Unmarked. SN 349. Gun retains 98% original nickel. Hammer screw a replacement. Very nice wood grips. Overall a sharp little gun and very clean $135*

Now take a look at the 1977 ad:

> *9 8686 - REMINGTON .22 CALIBER VEST POCKET DERRINGER. Serial number 349. Unmarked as is common. Nickel plated and about 98% remains. A few scratches by the hammer screw. Very nice plain walnut grips. Sharp . . $295*

I am convinced that we are talking about just one Vest Pocket Pistol. However, at this time, we are not able to ascertain what caliber it is.

Please note the numerous similarities found in these two advertisements:

1. Each of these Vest Pocket Pistols is described as having 98% nickel finish.
2. Both have "very nice" wood (walnut) grips.
3. Both of these guns were graded as being "sharp."
4. One hammer screw is described in one ad as a replacement, while coincidentally the other ad points out that there are "a few scratches" by the hammer screw.

There are just too many similarities here to accept as fact that there were two weapons in two different calibers with the same serial number. Except for the caliber, it appears as though both ads were describing the same pistol. Were there really two Remington Vest Pocket Pistols with the serial number 349? Or perhaps a typographical error had been made in one of the ads? Or maybe one bore was measured at the breech end and the other was measured at the muzzle end? (To understand just what this comment implies, see Chapter Four.) Possibly, someone guessed incorrectly!

Considering the serial number information gathered in this project, it is highly unlikely that the same serial number was intentionally given to two different-sized Remington Vest Pocket Pistols. So, the mystery lingers, because we still haven't been able to determine whether this incident is about one gun or two.

If there is only one serial number 349, does it belong to a .22 caliber or does it belong to a .32 caliber model? Unless "Lady Luck" intervenes and we are able to locate the current owner (or owners), we may never be able to discover the answer to this one.

- Serial number 159 has been reported in both .30 caliber and in .32 caliber. With the track record we have experienced with individuals attempting to determine the caliber of their No. 2 Size Vest Pocket Pistols, we might be talking about the same pistol.
- Serial number 362 shows up as a .41 caliber in *The Deringer in America, Volume II*, Eberhart/Wilson. Illustrated in color, between pages 96 and 97.
- The same number 362 was reported on a .30 caliber model, as well. (The owner of the .30 caliber weapon, is being contacted to see if this can be cleared up).
- Serial number C564 appears on a .22 caliber Vest Pocket. This entry is from a list submitted by a dealer who had collected Remington Vest Pocket Pistols for years. This serial number showed up again on a .41 caliber model, but without a prefix.
- Serial number 767 has been reported as the serial number of a .30 caliber and appears in the Moldenhauer Collection Book (#205) as .32 caliber, too. (A volunteer fax message from the owner solved this one, he owns "both" pistols… "It is a .30 caliber Remington Vest Pocket Pistol!" He thought he was buying a .32 caliber Vest Pocket, but inspection after the purchase revealed the true caliber. Time and response had paid off again…)

…Another Duplicate Set of Serial Numbers Has Been Eliminated!

- Serial number 1730 has been reported in .22 caliber, but with a prefix of "B" on the underside of the barrel. Serial number 1730 was also reported on a .32 caliber, without a prefix of any kind. Serial number 1730 (without the prefix "B") submitted on the .32 caliber has been verified.
- Serial number 3050 appeared twice, once on a .22 caliber Vest Pocket with a prefix of "R", while the same number 3050 was found an a .41 caliber pistol without any prefix.

Analyzing the information that had been submitted and consulting with my "Computer Guru," Jim Bivins, this very convincing working hypothesis has been developed:

Remington used a single consecutive series of serial numbers for their Vest Pocket Pistols, in all four calibers they produced.

The serial number spread reported is fairly consistent from #1 up through #15129. The next higher number reported is #16824. A big jump then occurs to #26543; next is a large gap up to #41880 (which has been verified). From there we experience another giant leap up to #70095. (This number is suspect, even though it came out of a museum's files. A request has been made for a physical verification).

The highest serial number reported is #84575. (This serial number appeared in The Rock Island Auction Catalog of November 1996, Lot #8. The auction house verified the serial number (over the phone and it was recorded.)

In view of these recent findings, the present owner is being sought. The number 8 prior to the 4575 might just be a well-worn prefix of "B". A quick look under the left grip could solve this, or maybe just add to the dilemma. We have no record of any prefixes having been found on the grip frame, just on the underside of the barrel, and then only on a very few .22 caliber models.

The majority of the serial numbers submitted and/or observed were found under the barrel and/or under the left grip. There were only nine Remington Vest Pocket Pistols reported (during the two surveys) without any serial numbers on them. (Five No. 1 Size, .22s; two No. 3 Size, .41 cal., and two Wire-Stocked Buggy/Bicycle Pocket Rifles). A look under the grips of these pistols might change these statistics.

A few of the submissions had a letter prefix. (There were five capitalized "B" prefixes, four "C", one "D", one "O" and four "R" prefixes on .22 caliber Vest Pocket Pistols and one Ampersand [&] prefix reportedly found on a .41 caliber Vest Pocket Model, serial #112). As mentioned before, prefix letters appeared only under the barrel, but none have been reported as having been found under the left grip on the frame.

In a few instances, the serial number under the barrel did not match the serial number on the frame, under the left grip. This leads to the conclusion that the pistol had been assembled using parts from two or more different guns.

Doug Eberhart told me that he subscribes to the single series of sequential serial numbers theory. He also said he thinks that if any serial numbers were duplicated, they were the result of factory errors. I certainly agree with that.

Attempting to verify the serial number sequencing, to identify the characteristics and idiosyncracies of these diminutive Vest Pocket Remingtons is, to say the least, challenging. Progress has been slow, but the results have been rewarding, making the effort all worthwhile.

My conclusions have been presented to some of those collectors who have provided so much assistance to me. Their contributions are a big part of this study. I respect their opinions and have attempted to incorporate their views in this effort.

Though some of the Vest Pockets were reported with no serial number on the underside of the barrel, virtually every Vest Pocket Pistol submitted in the survey had a serial number under the left grip on the toe of the frame. Serial numbers started with "1" and ran all the way to "84575". There are still some very large gaps in the sequence that need to be explained.

Reviewing the first 344 serial numbers encountered during this endeavor revealed these very perplexing findings:

> Within the first 1,000 serial numbers, 105 have been reported, that is 30.5% of the first 344 samples in this study.
> The second 1,000 serial numbers — 58 reported, 16.9%
> The third 1,000 — 46 reported, reflecting 13.4%
> The fourth 1,000 — 24 reported 7.0%
> The fifth 1,000 — 31 reported, 9.0%
> The sixth 1,000 — 6 reported, 0.17%
> The seventh 1,000 — 3 reported, 0.8%
> The eighth 1,000 — 12 reported, 3.4%
> The ninth 1,000 — 8 reported, 2.3%
> The tenth 1,000 — 4 reported, 0.4%
> The eleventh 1,000 — 8 reported, 2.3%
> The twelfth 1,000 — 5 reported, 1.45%
> The thirteenth 1,000 — 10 reported, 2.9%
> The fourteenth 1,000 — 4 reported, 1.16%
> The fifteenth 1,000 — 7 reported, 2.0%
> Then of the next 68,575, only an additional 7, (2.0%) were reported.

These numbers immediately provoke several questions:

1. How did the first owners realize that these Remington Vest Pocket Pistols would become collector's items?
2. Wouldn't it seem likely that the Vest Pocket Pistols built near the end of their production run would be more readily available today, being newer?
3. Why don't we find a more linear distribution of found-and-reported Vest Pocket Pistols or, better yet, at least a closer adherence to the normal distribution curve?

There are still many questions to be answered. The findings of this research contained in this volume, coupled with a few charts, illustrations and photographs, should provide fuel for stimulating conversation at future gun shows, RSA meetings and/or through e-mail contact.

An interesting incident occurred during the serial number search. Having seen Remington Vest Pocket Pistols advertised in previous issues of The Rock Island Auction Company catalogs, I paid a visit to their offices. Pat Hogan very graciously invited me to go through all of their catalogs. I hinted that someday maybe he would like to donate a full set of his catalogs to the Remington Society Research Group. Without hesitation he instructed one of his employees to box up a set so I could just take them with me.

Research certainly has some beneficial side effects. People treat you just like one of the family. They are eager to help in any way they can. So, if you have a pet Remington and can't readily find out very much about it, consider starting a research project of "your very own." It will not be simply a weekend activity, and I can guarantee you that it will keep you quite busy. You will also find it to be truly rewarding.

Subsequent to the spring 1999 auction at Rock Island, a startling discovery occurred. When the .41 caliber Vest Pocket Pistol I had just purchased was recorded on the research spreadsheet, its serial number duplicated that of a .32 caliber Vest Pocket Pistol already listed. A telephone call to the owner has confirmed that the serial number of 958 does, in fact, appear on both pistols. Here again, when you ask a Remington collector for information or verification of previously reported information, they happily respond. Such cooperation makes this type of effort a whole lot easier.

The information contained in this chapter was originally written as an article, which was presented to the *Remington Society of America Journal* and appeared in the second quarter issue of 1999.

An e-mail message popped up on my computer from William James Lawrence. Here is what Bill had to say in response to that article:

• • •

Subject: Remington Vest Pocket Serial Number Research
Date: Mon, 2 Aug 1999 15:07:16 - 0500 (EST)
From: William James Lawrence <wlawrenc@indiana.edu>
To: bobhat@lakeozarks.net
Hello Mr. Hatfield.

Having just finished reading your survey "status report" in the "JOURNAL", I thought I'd pass on the following for what it's worth. So far you've identified the letters "B", "C", "D", "O", and "R" as having been used as serial number prefixes. If memory serves (and I can't cite the source, though I think it was a RemShots query some years ago regarding a Remington # 4 rifle), Remington used letters from "BLACKPOWDER" as a date code for some of its products, no letter for "January", "B" for "February", ---, and "R" for "December". But I also seem to remember that this coding was discussed only with reference to what we generally call boys rifles and, further, that it may have only been used in the 1930's. But even if that were true, the same, very suitable word might have been used similarly even decades earlier, especially for another series of guns whose production patterns and bookkeeping requirements did not necessitate more rigid serial numbering.

I'll look forward to reading your next installment, and I wish you and all those helping you the best of luck.

Bill Lawrence
Life Member, RSA, ASSRA, and so forth

• • •

His e-mail message was received the very same day I received my copy of that issue of the *Journal* in the mail. Please note the theory he advanced concerning the prefixes found on some of the Remington Vest Pocket Pistols. Sorry Bill, I can't endorse that one. This e-mail message was immediately sent to Roy Marcot, *RSA Journal* Editor, letting him know just how rapidly the *RSA Journal* had provoked a response from one of its readers.

• • •

```
Subject: [Fwd: Remington Vest Pocket Serial Number Research]
Date: Mon, 02 Aug 1999 15:38:17 -0500
From: "Robert E. Hatfield" <bobhat@mail.lakeozarks.net>
Organization: Hatfield, LTD
To: roymarcot@email.msn.com
CC: lwierjr@aol.com

Roy: Here's proof that your RSA Journal really does the job.
Best regards, BOB
```

• • •

Bill Lawrence's e-mail message was included in the message to Roy as an attachment. This testimonial to the effectiveness of the *Journal* of the Remington Society of America was just too great not to share. A copy of this correspondence was, of course, shared with Ol' RemShots, too!

Talk about effectiveness. The very next day, Dick Littlefield called from New Hampshire. During our phone conversation, he furnished an additional thirty Remington Vest Pocket serial numbers. They had been collected and logged over the past five years. Some of these numbers had been submitted previously. Seventeen of them were .22 caliber, and four were .30 caliber (all with brass frames). Additionally, there were three .32 caliber and the remaining six serial numbers were .41 caliber models.

This input provided nearly a ten percent increase to the serial number base for this research. Dick said that the survival rate of 19th-century firearms was between five and eight percent, today. He went on to explain that these percentages would be uniformly found for the years they were produced. Dick compared Marlin's serial numbering with what he has discovered about Remington. He commented that he felt that there was more than one series of sequential Vest Pocket serial numbers.

Next, a fax was received from Antioch, Illinois. It was from the owner of the Vest Pocket Pistol with serial number 767. He cleared up the conflict surrounding this serial number, as was previously discussed.

Strangely enough, the first three reactions to the publication of the article in the *RSA Journal*, "Single Series of Sequential Serial Numbers for All Calibers Collectively" each employed a different means of communications. E-mail came in from Indiana, a telephone call originated in New Hampshire and then a fax was received from Illinois. All in a period of less than two days.

Looking back to the period of time when Remington was manufacturing Vest Pocket Pistols during the Civil War and shortly thereafter, only the telegraph system was available for "speedy" communications. Western Union, whose lines ran east to west, and American Telegraph, whose lines ran north and south, made up the telegraph system in the United States. There were telegraph offices in most major cities throughout the country.

People in small rural communities the size of Lake Ozark, Missouri (which incidentally was not even in existence then), would not have enjoyed the luxury of such "modern technology" as the telegraph system. I am certainly grateful for all of our modern communications technologies and the interested Remington collectors who make use of them. The interest shown and the sharing attitudes displayed by *RSA Journal* readers is most gratifying.

Before leaving the serial number subject, let's take another look at that production-dating indicator **"B - L - A - C - K - P - O - W - D - E - R "** system suggestion that Bill Lawrence had referred to in his e-mail message. The theory was that Remington used this "code word" to indicate the month of the year the weapons were produced and would have worked like this:

There was no letter used for January. (So, if no letter prefix were present, the pistol was manufactured in January).

B would be used for February,
L would have indicated March,
A would point out April production,
C would illustrate guns built in May,
K was the prefix to show June production,
P indicated guns made in July,
O would have served as an indication the pistol was built during August,
W was used for September,
D for October,
E would signify November,
R would then designate December production.

Would the existence of this type of date-coding system (during the generally accepted period of the Civil War through 1888, when the Remington Vest Pocket Pistols were produced) indicate that the people at Remington were clairvoyant? Of course not, but Remington management was certainly aware of the development of gun-cotton (an early attempt to make smokeless powder) around the 1840s. The Remington Vest Pocket Pistols were designed to use black powder, or at least light loads. So, it is not totally impossible to accept the thought that a system of this sort could have been used. Was Remington preparing for faster burning and smokeless powder with the black powder system serving as a warning not to use any other propellant in Vest Pockets?

When viewing and reviewing J. Wayne Matthews' annual production chart for the Remington over/under double-barrel derringer, the date coding theory shows up again. The major difference is that he indicates "**B - L - A - C - K - P - O - W - D - E - R - X**" ("B" for January, with "X" being the December prefix). Letters show up on the third and fourth models.

Even though his chart spells out that production-bearing letters are for the period 1888 to 1935, it bears mentioning, because 1888 was about the time production of the Remington Vest Pocket Pistols came to a screeching halt. If such a system were used on the Vest Pockets, there are a number of unanswered questions that leap into mind, e.g.:

- Why have so few samples of the Remington Vest Pocket Pistol art been found with letter prefixes coupled with the pistols' serial numbers?
- When a letter prefix was used, just what did it signify?
- Why have letter prefixes been found only on .22 caliber Vest Pockets?
- Is my Vest Pocket Pistol with a prefix more valuable or a more desirable collectible than a similar one without a prefix...or vice versa? If so, why?

Questions like these force this effort to become an ongoing study!

Just when this chapter appeared to be complete, Larry Moody called to share information and photographs of a pair of cased and engraved .22 caliber Remington Vest Pocket Pistols. The pair is cased, complete with an ivory cleaning rod.

Larry feels that this may be the Deluxe Set of its time. As you peruse the photograph, consider:

- A strange feature about this decorative duo is the gigantic gap between the serial numbers. Larry conveyed the two serial numbers as: "315" and "12667".

***The Gamblers (Old West)*, Time-Life Books, indicated that this set is most unusual, because the guns were usually sold singly.** (Cased set of Remington Vest Pocket Pistols from RSA member Larry Moody Collection. Photograph by Drew Moody)

- Serial numbers that far apart make it difficult to accept that this is a factory cased set.
- One would assume that if it were, the serial numbers would be consecutive, or at least reasonably close.
- The high serial numbered pistol could be a replacement for a lost original, or the set could have been put together by some after-market provider.
- The sign in the top of the box indicates that the pair were cased by A. Fleishhacker & Co., 532 Market St., San Francisco, in February of 1892.
- The photograph reveals that the grip screws, for example, have been positioned differently.

There is still another strange facet of this serial number story. As previously mentioned, the lower of the two serial numbers was reported to have been "315." I have a .22 caliber Remington Vest Pocket Pistol with a serial number of "315." This "strange" duplication surfaced when these two numbers were checked against the master serial number spreadsheet. The three individual

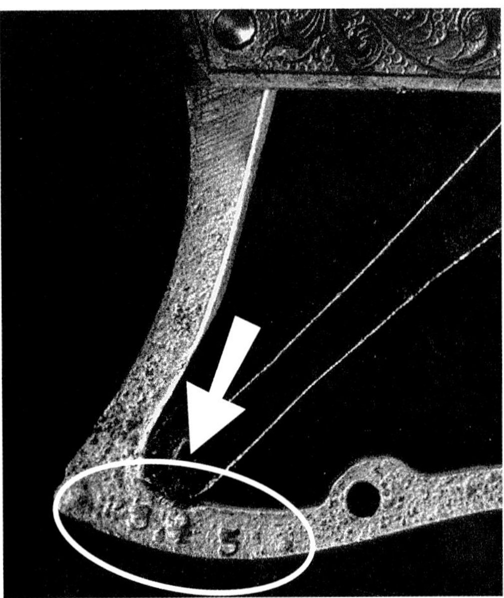

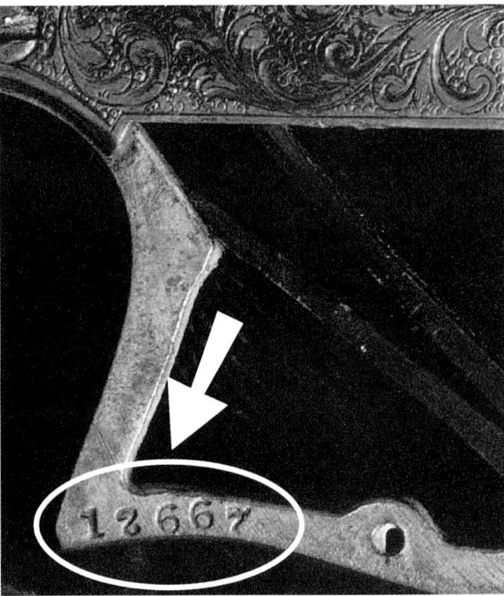

(Above, left) **Right-side view of Vest Pocket Pistol, SN345.** *(Above, right)* **Left-side view of grip frame, SN12667.** (RSA member Larry Moody Collection. Photo by Drew Moody)

numbers are crisp and clear, and each number is equidistant from the numbers adjacent to it. It is quite unlikely that Remington built two separate .22 Vest Pocket Pistols with the same serial number. Take a close look at the photo.

Subsequent inspection, of the "315" pistol from the cased set revealed that the first number, "3" is reasonably distinguishable and the last number, "5" is crisp and clear.

However, the center number, thought to have been a "1" was placed on a rough surface area, making that number difficult to read. Even under a magnifying glass, one cannot be sure if it is a "1" or a "4". Close inspection of the central digit shows a small horizontal line about halfway up the vertical marking. Sure could be a "4". Of course, the resulting serial number of "345" would ease all of the concern.

Serial number 12667 in the photo above is located close to the toe of the left side of the grip frame. This is where the majority of serial numbers are found on Remington Vest Pocket Pistols.

Chapter Three

How Many Were Manufactured?

Preliminary research indicated that we really don't know just how many Remington Vest Pocket Pistols were actually manufactured. This effort does shed some light on estimates of the quantities Remington produced. A thorough search of numerous printed sources does indicate that the best-guess scenario appears to be that approximately 25,000 were manufactured in .22 caliber alone.

Published estimates of the quantities built by Remington in the larger No. 2 and No. 3 Sizes range from approximately 10,000 to a combined sum equal to the amount produced in .22 caliber. Using the larger of those estimates, that approximately 25,000 additional Vest Pocket Pistols were produced in the larger sizes, would elevate the overall estimate of production by Remington in all calibers to approximately 50,000.

K.D. Kirkland's estimates were: 25,000 in .22 caliber and approximately 10,000 in the split-breech larger models. Leon Wier has suggested that Remington manufactured 25,000 plus .22 caliber Vest Pocket Pistols, and an additional 10,000 in .30 and .41 calibers combined. Robert W.D. Ball also estimated that there were 10,000 built in .30, .32 and .41 calibers combined.

In May 1997, a letter was received from Jim Shaffer of Irwin, Pennsylvania. He has been tracking Remington Vest Pocket serial numbers for more than 30 years. Those numbers are included in this research.

Jim's initial correspondence has been reproduced as Appendix 9 on page 110. The serial numbers he observed and recorded at gun shows, in catalogs, auction lists and books led him to the following conclusions:

TOTAL PRODUCTION OF REMINGTON VEST POCKET PISTOLS (all calibers)
Ranges from 25,800 to 28,300

.22 caliber total production — about 15,000
.30 caliber total production — about 2,800
.32 caliber total production — 3,000 to 3,500
.41 caliber total production — about 5,000

Most sources, however, tend to agree that there were approximately 25,000 Remington Vest Pocket Pistols manufactured in .22 caliber. One source (Madaus '97) indicated that only about 16,500 were made in .22 caliber. Harold Peterson suggested that a grand total of 50,000 Vest Pockets were made by Remington in all four calibers.

Alden Hatch put the total at 25,000 plus. Ned Schwing and Herb Houze surmised that 25,000 were produced in .22 caliber and 10,000 in split-breech models, a combination of .30, .32 and .41 calibers.

Flayderman's Guide... established production figures at: 25,000 in .22 caliber Vest Pocket Pistols plus 10,000 or less in the other three calibers. There is general agreement that approximately 10,000 Remington Vest Pocket Pistols were made in No. 2 Size and No. 3 Size collectively. The .30 caliber and the .32 caliber models constitute the No. 2 Size category.

The dates of manufacture and the quantity estimate data found in Appendices 1 and 2 (see pg. 85) illustrate the estimates made by writers/researchers in the past. Most estimates tend to reinforce the "Single Serial Number Theory" advanced in Chapter Two.

There you have it (by consensus):
Remington produced 15,000 or maybe 16,500, or maybe 25,000, or maybe even more Vest Pocket Pistols in .22 caliber rimfire short... The production totals of the larger-bore split-breech models...were collectively narrowed down to something less than 10,000, or maybe it was 10,000, or perhaps even 16,500, or could that have been 25,000, or perhaps more!

Actually, the majority of sources agree with the total production of approximately 25,000 Remington Vest Pocket Pistols in .22 caliber and about 10,000, more or less, of the larger, split-breech models. (.30, .32 and .41 calibers combined).

How many Total Vest Pocket Pistols did Remington actually manufacture?

Analyzing the serial number data collected and advancing a few assumptions may just confuse the issue even more. Here are three different approaches to the question:

METHOD NO. 1:

Assuming the following:

a. Each caliber had its own series of consecutive serial numbers, starting with Number 1.
b. That "ALL" serial numbers in this study are valid.
c. Every serial number was used.

Based on the above criteria, total production, by caliber, would have amounted to:

Caliber	Serial # Range Reported		Probable Total
.22	1–84,575		84,575
.30	2–10,790		10,790
.32	40–3,513		3,513
.41	13–10,866		10,866
		Grand Total	109,744

Using Method No. 1...
The "Total Vest Pocket Pistol Production" would have tremendously exceeded any and all of the "Estimated Production Totals" that we have encountered to date!

METHOD NO. 2:

Assuming the following:

a. That a separate series of sequential serial numbers was used for each size of Vest Pocket Pistol, starting with number 1 in each size. (Size No. 1 — .22 caliber, Size No. 2 — .30 and .32 calibers combined, and Size No. 3 — .41 caliber)
b. That "ALL" serial numbers in this study are valid.
c. That every serial number was used.

Based on this modified criteria, Remington Vest Pocket Pistol production would have been:

Caliber	Serial # Range Reported		Probable Total
.22 (No. 1 Size)	1–84,575		84,575
.30 & .32 (No. 2 Size)	2–10,790		10,790
.41 (No. 3 Size)	13–10,866		10,866
		Grand Total	**106,231**

Using Method No. 2...
When you figure the estimated Vest Pocket Pistol production this way, the grand total still exceeds all expectations.

METHOD NO. 3:

This time we will assume:

a. That Remington used only one series of consecutive serial numbers for all of their Vest Pocket Pistols, regardless of caliber, starting with the number 1. (That single series of sequential serial numbers I've been talking about.)
b. We are also assuming that "ALL" of the serial numbers encountered in this study are valid.
c. Also, that all numbers were used.

Using Method No. 3...
Since the sequence started with Serial Number 1, and the largest serial number encountered during this study was 84,575, the production would have to have been at least 84,575!

Considering the percentage of each caliber, based on the frequency of their appearance during this study of a sampling containing 362 specimens, we find:

- The 174 reported in .22 caliber accounts for about 48% of the total. Approximately 12% of the entries were reported to have been .30 caliber models, represented by 42 pistols.

- Based on the 30 submissions in .32 caliber Vest Pockets, they account for slightly more than 8%.
- One hundred and three additional pistols, representing 28% of the total reflect the .41 caliber segment of the study.
- The remaining nearly 4% were the thirteen long-barrel/buggy rifles reported.

These facts and figures will probably be a little easier to digest when illustrated in chart form. (Take a look at Appendix 3 on page 86.)

Now, we are going to assume that the representation by caliber in this research effort also signifies the actual percentage of the total Remington Vest Pocket Pistol production. By doing this, we can project a reasonable estimate of production totals by caliber.

Caliber	Percent of Study Sampling	Probable Total
.22	48%	40,596
.30	12%	10,149
.32	8%	6,766
.41	28%	23,681
Buggy Rifle	4%	3,383
	100%	**84,575**

Regardless of how many Remington Vest Pocket Pistols were made in all the various individual models, sizes, calibers and configurations, and considering all the information at hand, the conclusion reached is:

Remington produced a grand total of approximately 85,000 Vest Pocket Pistols!

PUBLISHER'S NOTE — ANOTHER INTERPRETATION:

While inspecting the press proofs for this book, I thought of another way to interpret the serial number data, resulting in a very different figure for total production. When I called the author, he immediately said, "That's an interesting thought! Let's include it as an Editor's Note at the end of the chapter." Throughout this book, the author has often talked about the true spirit of research, where you keep an open mind rather than sticking to assumptions. This immediate eagerness to include a new interpretation, even if it is very different from his own, is a great example of what he is talking about.

On page 33, the author explains that there is a fairly regular distribution of serial numbers reported in the survey. After an initial spike (probably accounted for by proud collectors eager to report their early pistols), the rate of pistols reported settles down to about seven guns for each thousand serial numbers. But this all changes at the 16,000 mark. Between serial number 16,000 and serial number 84,575, only seven guns are reported — about as many as we would expect for each *thousand* within that span. But as the author points out, survival rates should be *higher* for later-production guns, not lower. How do we explain this? Unless Remington exported huge numbers of late guns (which seems unlikely), I suggest that *Remington might not have used all of the serial numbers after 16,000 for Vest Pocket Pistols.* Perhaps, after the initial popularity of the pistol died down, Remington started to produce them in small batches, and for convenience sake began each batch with a big round number, leaving most numbers unused. This system is documented for at least one other maker of small pistols. Or maybe, like on one Winchester model, they just skipped large chunks of numbers for some unknown reason. In any case, if we trust the survey's rate of seven guns reported per thousand produced, it seems possible that just 1,000 pistols were made after the 16,000 mark. **This gives a grand total of approximately 17,000 pistols,** which breaks down to 8,160 in .22; 2,040 in .30; 1,360 in .32; 4,760 in .41; and 680 buggy rifles. Lastly, since collectors seek rarities, I suspect that rare types get over-represented in surveys, which might alter these proportions, however slightly. — *Stuart Mowbray*

Chapter Four

What Calibers Were Produced?

At least one source intimated that Remington Vest Pocket Pistols were produced in *five* calibers: .22 caliber, .30 caliber, .32 caliber, .38 caliber and .41 caliber. As reported in the '97 monograph, I am still convinced that these little beauties were manufactured in only four calibers: .22, .30, .32 and .41, all rimfire short. Many sources do not even include all four of these. However, the survey forms submitted do confirm the existence of all four, and I am thoroughly convinced that these four calibers do exist and I possess proof positive. I have at least one of each in my collection.

Speculation about the manufacture of .38 caliber Remington Vest Pocket Pistols has never been substantiated. Occasionally, a reference to a .38 caliber Remington Vest Pocket Pistol rears its head. Generally, this can be neutralized by accurately measuring the bore and/or seating a .41 caliber rimfire short cartridge in the chamber. The two .41 caliber models in my collection measure approximately .37 and .38 calibers at the muzzle end of the bore, respectively. When measured at the breech, they both measure .41 caliber. A .41 rimfire short cartridge seats well in both.

While composing this chapter, I also spent a short while "surfing the net." Visiting Dixie Gun Works' web pages, I encountered a listing for a .38 caliber Remington Vest Pocket Pistol for sale. I immediately gave Dixie Gun Works a call, and they graciously agreed to physically pick up the advertised gun. Much to my dismay, when they did measure the bore, it measured .38 caliber.

Needless to say, I was about ready to hop in the car and drive to Union City, Tennessee. Common sense intervened, and a letter was rushed off to the folks at Dixie, requesting a recheck. They were asked to measure the bore at the breech end and to attempt to seat a .41 rimfire short round in the chamber, as mentioned earlier. Hoping my suspicions would be confirmed, and since I had been so certain that there were no .38 caliber Vest Pocket Pistols built by Remington for the retail market, I waited impatiently for a response.

To my knowledge, the only .38 caliber Remington Vest Pocket Pistol that existed was a factory prototype owned by Dr. Karl Spryidon of Ohio. (The search continues). Incidentally, this particular pistol was referred to as ".44 caliber split-breech derringer" in *The William M. Locke Collection.*

Talk about cooperation, Charles Kirkland at Dixie Gun Works received my letter and phoned me immediately. He reported that he had used the method that I had suggested in my letter to determine if measuring the bore at the breech and attempting to load a .41 caliber rimfire cartridge in the pistol would yield a different result.

Charles had measured the pistol's bore again, and sure enough it measured .41 caliber. A .41 caliber cartridge case did fit tightly in the chamber. Once again, the suspicion has failed to be proven that a .38 caliber Vest Pocket Pistol was manufacutured by Remington for the retail trade.

However, the cooperative spirit of the people at Dixie Gun Works has certainly been illustrated. Their concern for the truth and satisfying their customers has been evidenced by their special effort. With assistance like this, hopefully someday we will be able to unlock additional secrets concerning details about Remington's Vest Pocket Pistols.

Considering the 344 Remington Vest Pocket Pistols included in this research, if Remington had really manufactured .38 caliber Vest Pocket Pistols, why haven't some of them, or at least one of them, surfaced? Why haven't we found any evidence that Remington ever advertised that .38 caliber models were even an option?

Remember, some of the information available concerning Remington Vest Pocket Pistols does not even recognize the fact that there were four calibers produced. (Survey input verified that there were Remington Vest Pocket Pistols in only four calibers: .22 caliber, rimfire short; .30 caliber, rimfire short; .32 caliber, rimfire short and .41 caliber, rimfire short. Other than the aforementioned .38 caliber factory prototype, there is no evidence that Remington ever produced any for sale in that caliber.) Every incident suggesting Remington had produced .38 caliber Vest Pocket Pistols has been thoroughly investigated.

Some sources emphasize the "fact" that .30 caliber models were not built. Since a reasonable number of .30 caliber Vest Pockets were reported, coupled with the "fact" that this author is the proud owner of .22 caliber, .30 caliber, .32 caliber, as well as .41 caliber Remington Vest Pocket Pistols, it is not only reasonable and safe to assume but a proven fact that Remington did, in fact, build them. Just to reinforce this information, photographs of the alleged samples of these manufactured items are included in this volume.

Frequently, recent advertising for individual Remington Vest Pocket Pistols for sale has included the phrase "Rare, .30 caliber." Based on the numbers reported in the survey information received during this study, there were more .30 caliber models reported (forty-two of them) than .32 caliber models (only thirty). If this input represents a true cross-section of the Vest Pockets actually produced, the .32 caliber models are the rarer of the two. Obviously, it may be concluded from our research input that the .30 and the .32 caliber models did not share the popularity enjoyed by the .22 caliber and the .41 caliber models.

Remington designated three physical sizes for the Vest Pocket Pistols they produced:

a. The No. 1 Size Remington Vest Pocket Pistols (the smallest size they manufactured) were produced in .22 caliber only.

b. The No. 2 Size Remington Vest Pocket Pistols (this intermediate size being the only Vest Pocket size that was produced in more than one caliber), .30 caliber as well as .32 caliber were built utilizing the No. 2 Size frame. All of the No. 2 Size Remington Vest Pocket Pistols were split-breech models.

c. The No. 3 Size Remington Vest Pocket Pistol (the largest of the Remington Vest Pockets). This frame was used for .41 caliber Vest Pocket Pistols only.

Without proof to the contrary having been uncovered, the logical conclusion is that Remington produced Vest Pocket Pistols in three sizes and four calibers:

Size 1 in .22 caliber
Size 2 in .30 and .32 calibers
Size 3 in .41 caliber

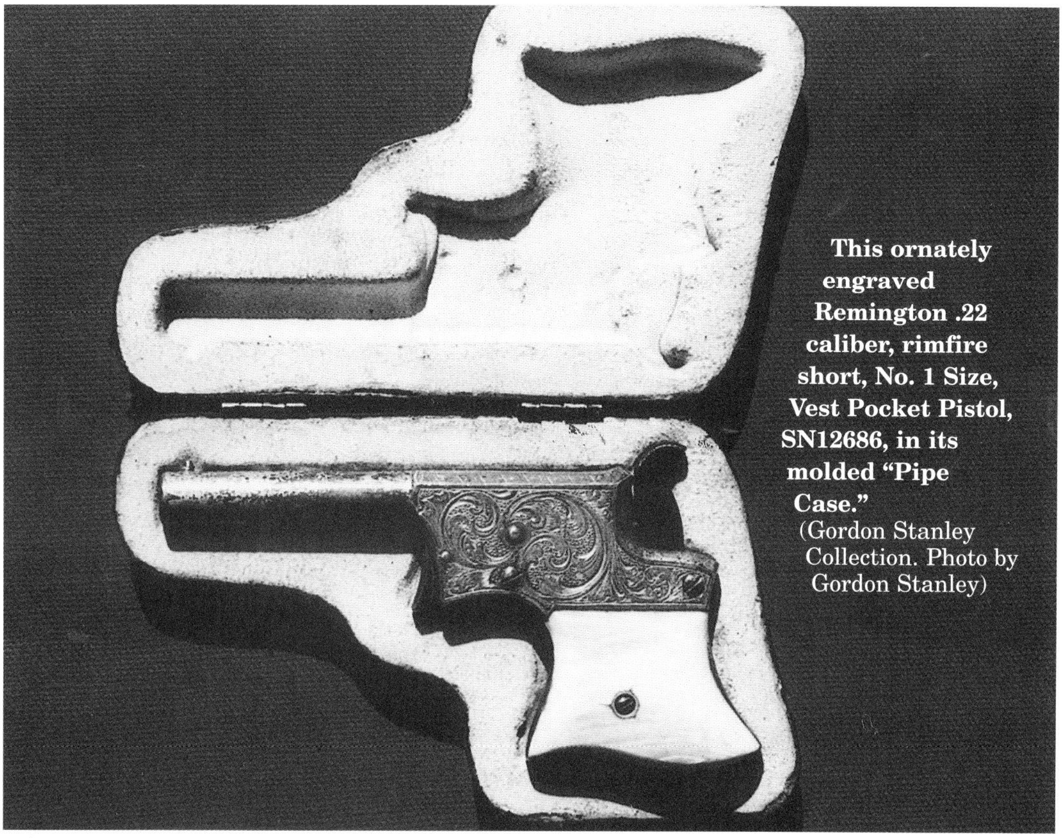

This ornately engraved Remington .22 caliber, rimfire short, No. 1 Size, Vest Pocket Pistol, SN12686, in its molded "Pipe Case."
(Gordon Stanley Collection. Photo by Gordon Stanley)

Remington Factory Prototype .38 caliber Vest Pocket Pistol.
(Dr. Karl Spryidon Collection. Photo by Dr. Spryidon)

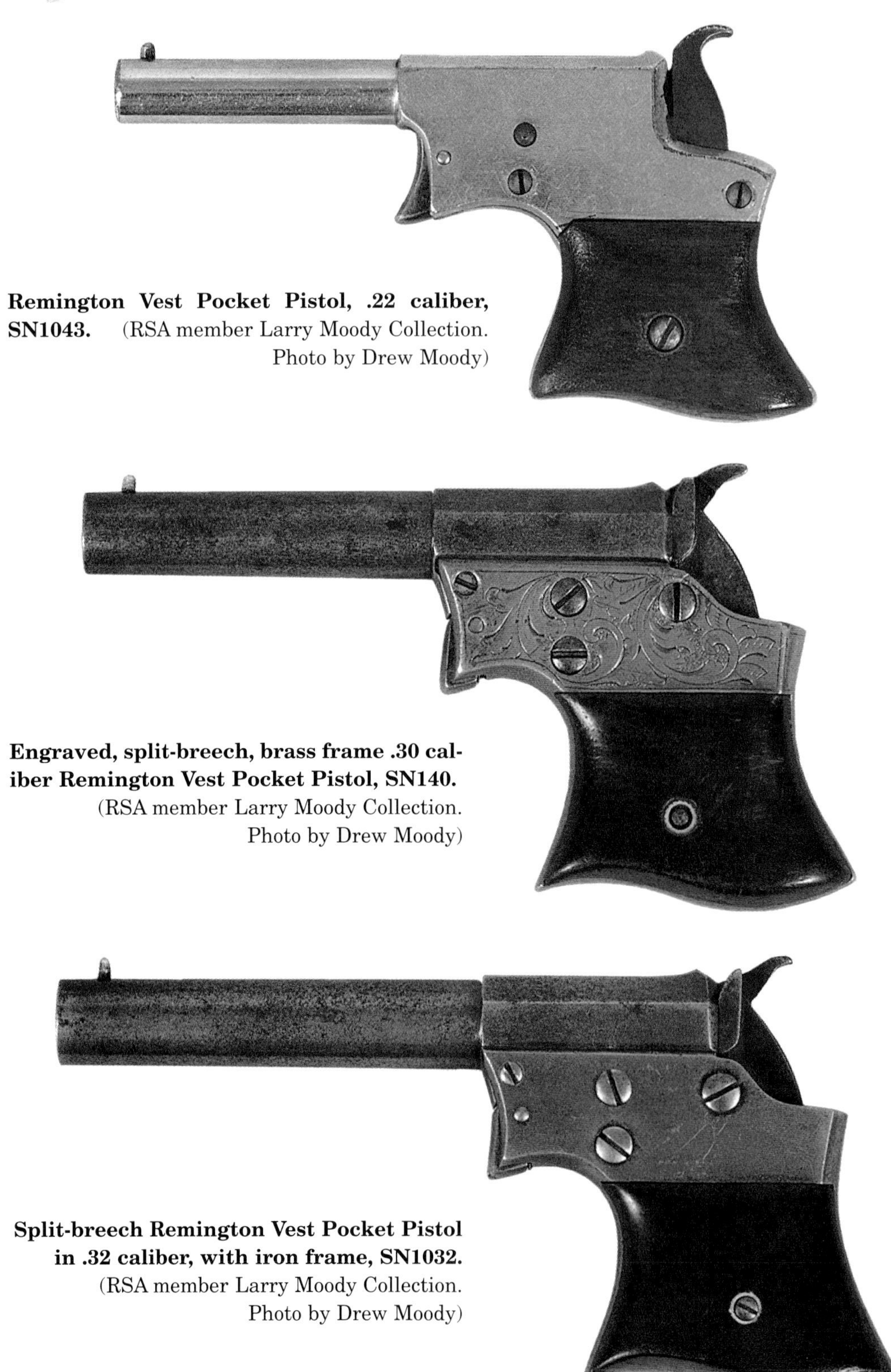

Remington Vest Pocket Pistol, .22 caliber, SN1043. (RSA member Larry Moody Collection. Photo by Drew Moody)

Engraved, split-breech, brass frame .30 caliber Remington Vest Pocket Pistol, SN140. (RSA member Larry Moody Collection. Photo by Drew Moody)

Split-breech Remington Vest Pocket Pistol in .32 caliber, with iron frame, SN1032. (RSA member Larry Moody Collection. Photo by Drew Moody)

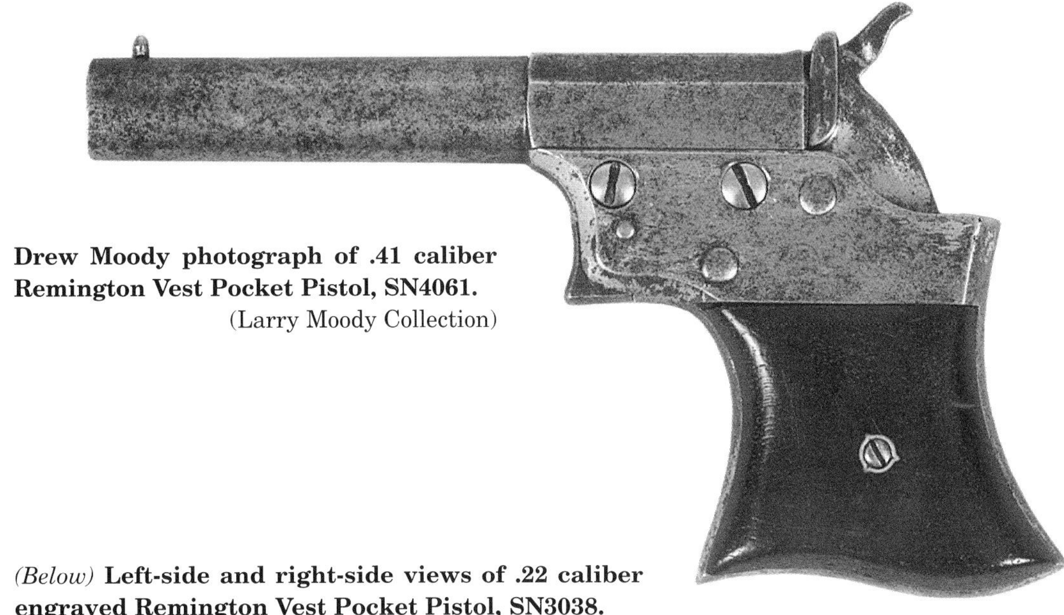

Drew Moody photograph of .41 caliber Remington Vest Pocket Pistol, SN4061.
(Larry Moody Collection)

(Below) **Left-side and right-side views of .22 caliber engraved Remington Vest Pocket Pistol, SN3038.**
(Mike Butler Photos)

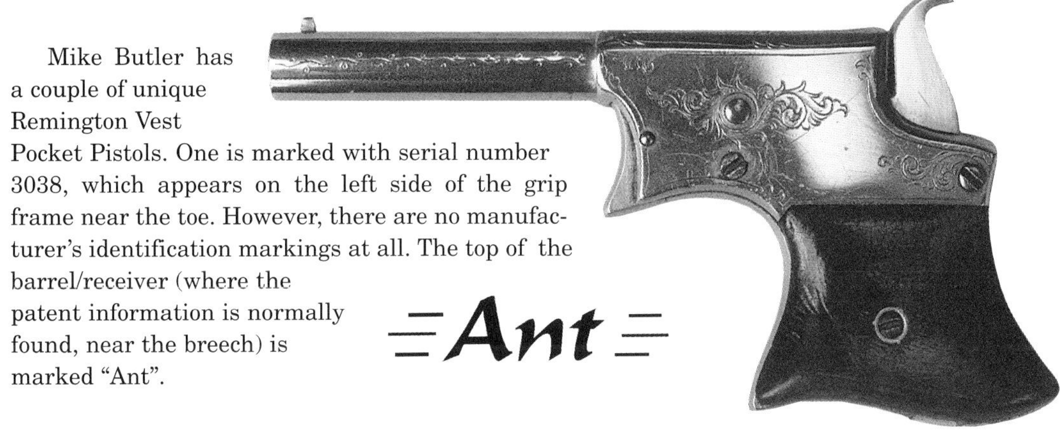

Mike Butler has a couple of unique Remington Vest Pocket Pistols. One is marked with serial number 3038, which appears on the left side of the grip frame near the toe. However, there are no manufacturer's identification markings at all. The top of the barrel/receiver (where the patent information is normally found, near the breech) is marked "Ant".

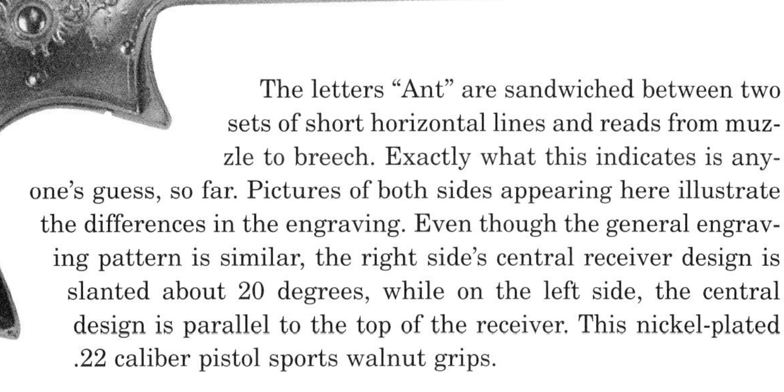

The letters "Ant" are sandwiched between two sets of short horizontal lines and reads from muzzle to breech. Exactly what this indicates is anyone's guess, so far. Pictures of both sides appearing here illustrate the differences in the engraving. Even though the general engraving pattern is similar, the right side's central receiver design is slanted about 20 degrees, while on the left side, the central design is parallel to the top of the receiver. This nickel-plated .22 caliber pistol sports walnut grips.

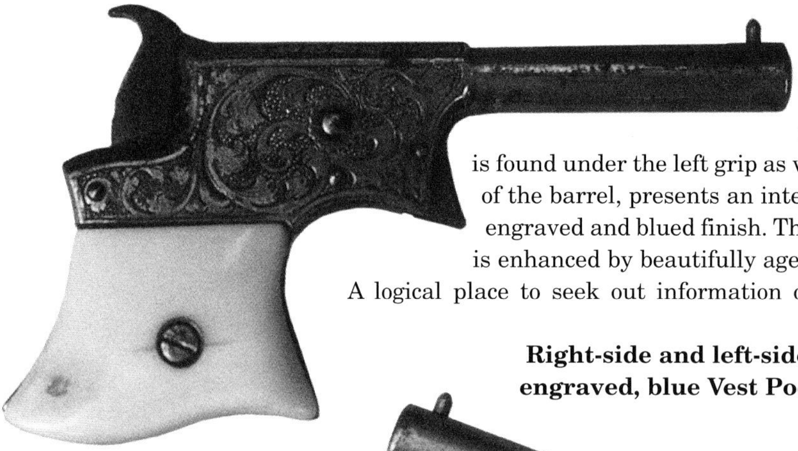

Another .22 caliber Mike Butler Vest Pocket Pistol, serial number 12610, which is found under the left grip as well as on the underside of the barrel, presents an interesting picture with its engraved and blued finish. The overall attractiveness is enhanced by beautifully aged ivory grips.

A logical place to seek out information on Remington firearms of any type was the Remington Arms Museum, in Ilion, New York. Members of the Remington Society of America Research Team visited the Remington Arms facility in October 2000. During that visit, valuable research information was gathered.

Right-side and left-side views of .22 caliber engraved, blue Vest Pocket Pistol, SN12610. (Mike Butler Photo)

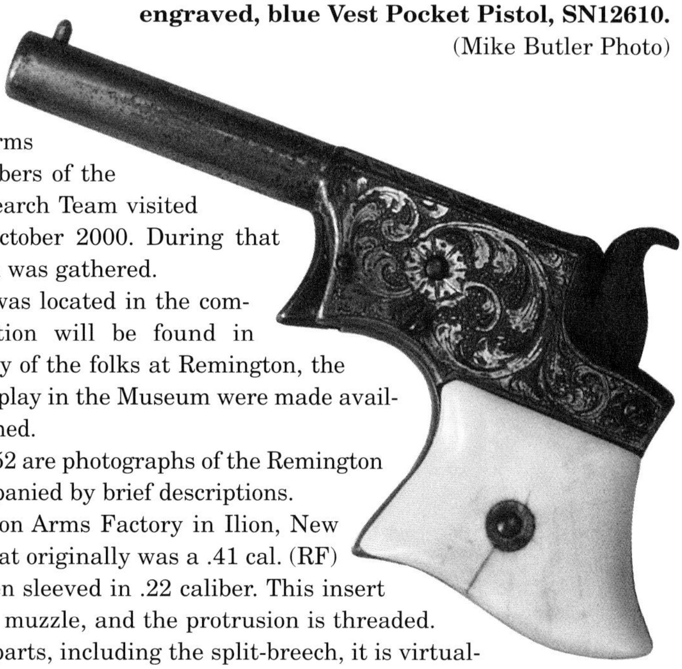

Additional patent information was located in the company's archives. Patent information will be found in Appendix 8. Through the hospitality of the folks at Remington, the Vest Pocket Pistols that were on display in the Museum were made available to be inspected and photographed.

Below and on pages 49 through 52 are photographs of the Remington Museum Vest Pocket Pistols accompanied by brief descriptions.

In the archives of the Remington Arms Factory in Ilion, New York, there is a No. 3 Size frame that originally was a .41 cal. (RF) short Vest Pocket Pistol. It has been sleeved in .22 caliber. This insert extends 3/16 of an inch beyond the muzzle, and the protrusion is threaded. Since the weapon is missing some parts, including the split-breech, it is virtually impossible to determine any logical reason for the modifications.

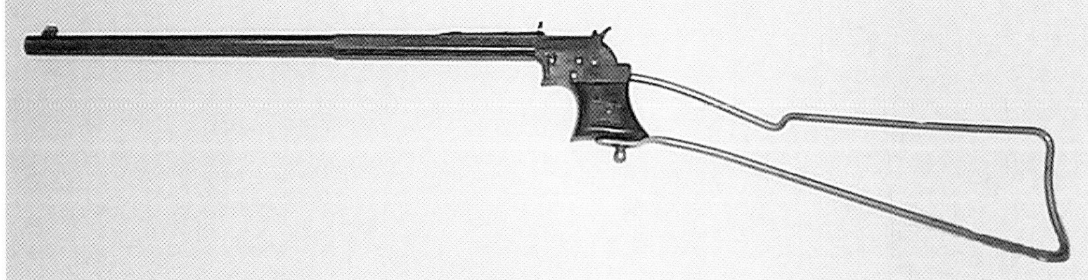

Remington Vest Pocket Pistol, SN1338, was built on a No. 2 Size frame. The barrel is .22 caliber and is 15-1/4 inches in length. The original finish is blue and the grips are walnut. The detachable stock is held in place by a knurled knob, while the retaining knob on SN3828 (pictured on page 51) resembles a fitting for a lanyard ring. There doesn't appear to have been any two of the longer barreled so-called Vest Pocket Buggy rifles configured totally the same. (Bob Hatfield Photo)

Remington Vest Pocket Pistols in the Remington Arms Museum • October 2000

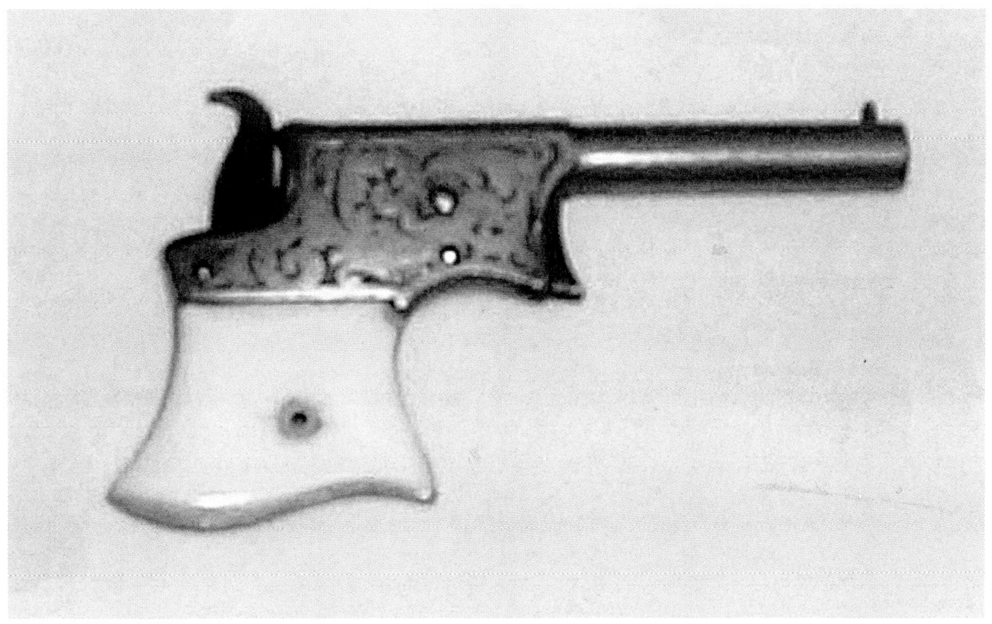

View of the right side of Remington Vest Pocket Pistol .22 cal. (RF) short, SN12898. Beautifully engraved with aged ivory grips. (Bob Hatfield Photo)

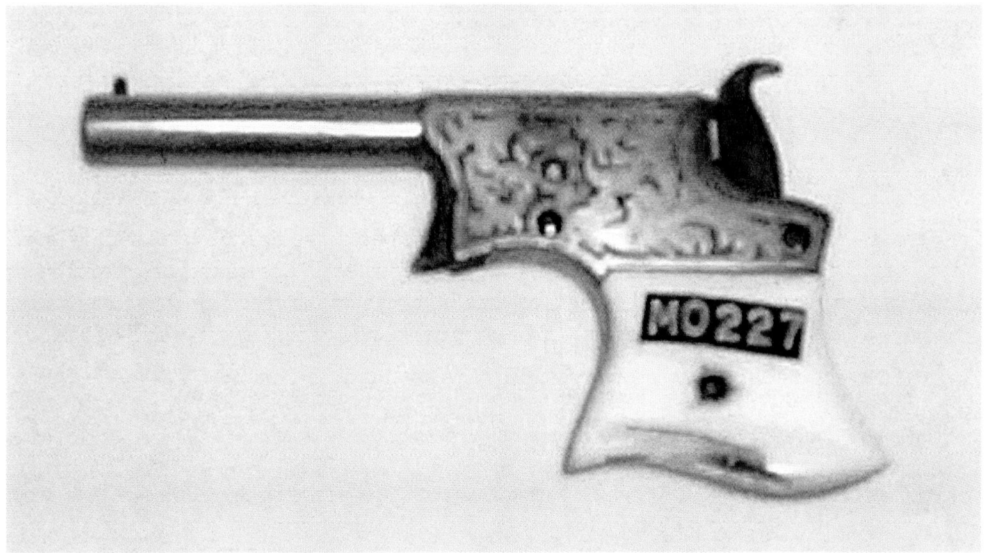

View of the left side of Remington Vest Pocket Pistol .22 cal. (RF) short, SN12898. (Bob Hatfield Photo)

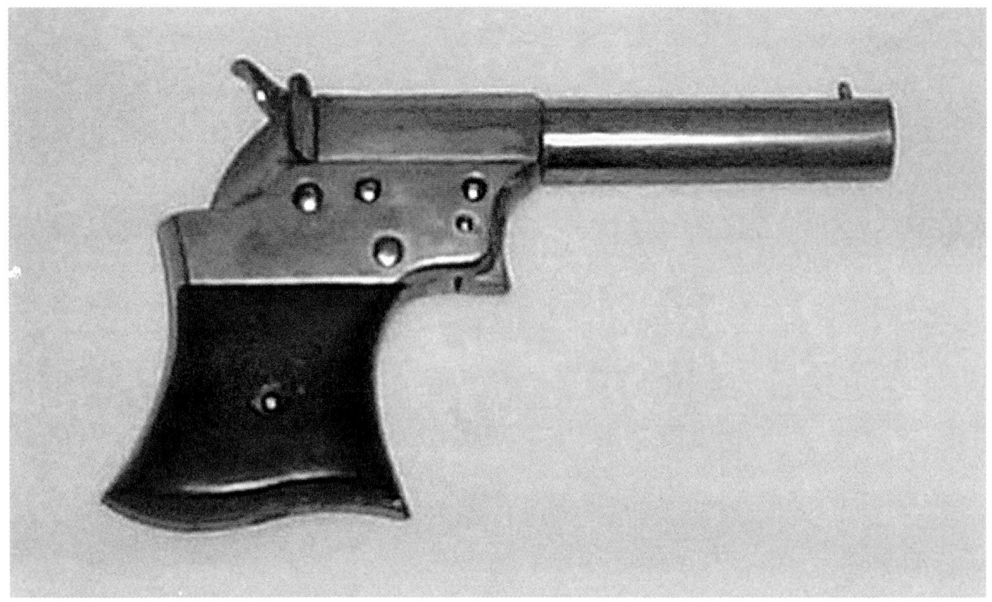

Right-side view of Remington Vest Pocket Pistol, SN2415. Originally the finish was blue. The grips are walnut. (Bob Hatfield Photo)

Left side of the same Remington Vest Pocket Pistol, SN2415. (Bob Hatfield Photo)

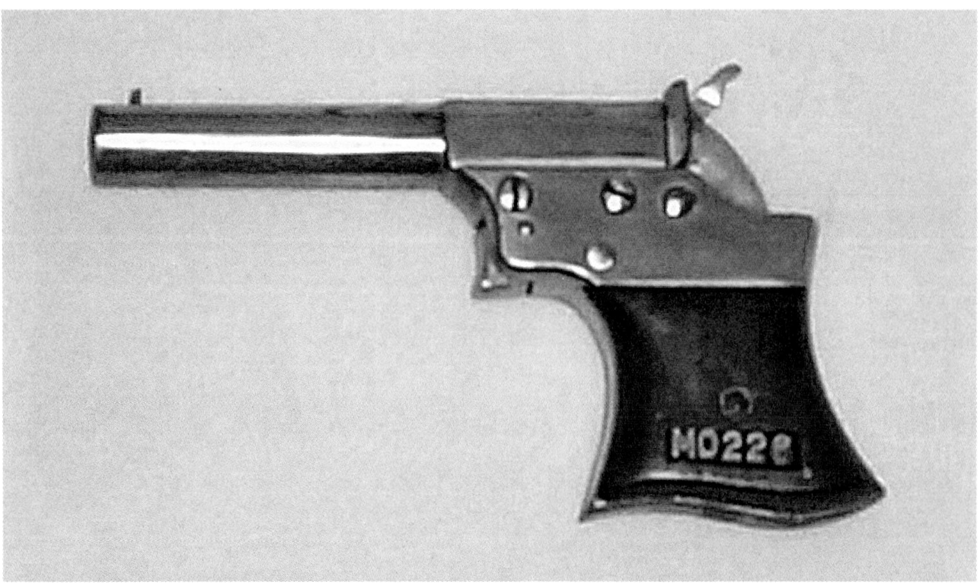

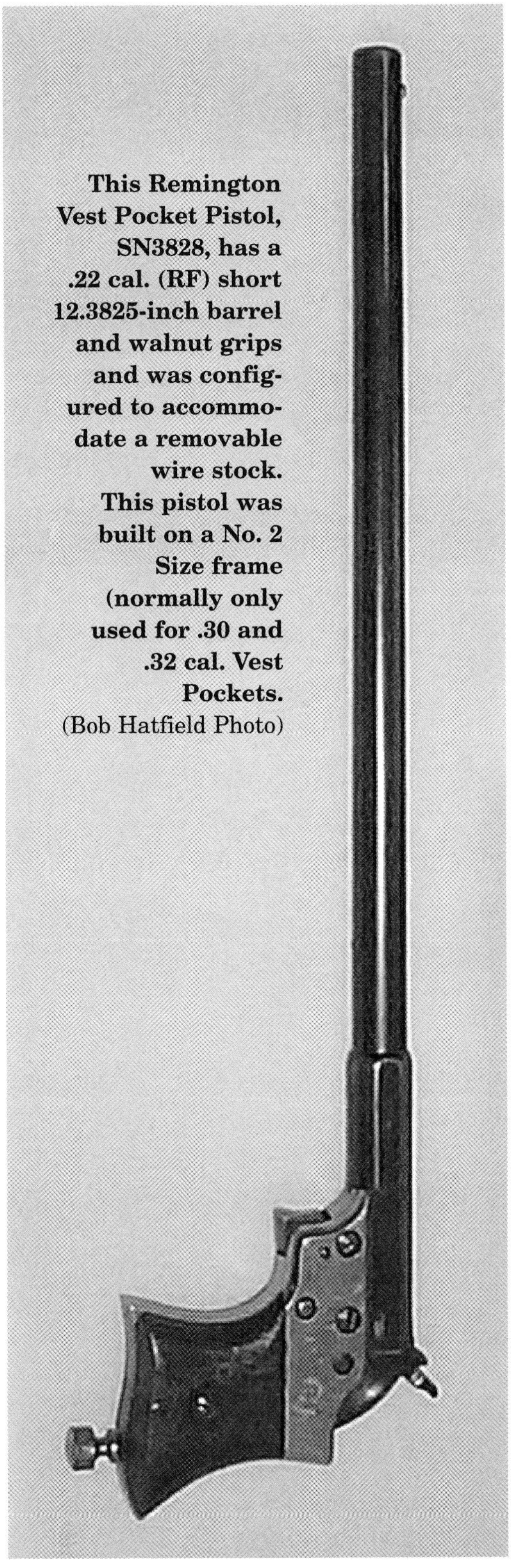

This Remington Vest Pocket Pistol, SN3828, has a .22 cal. (RF) short 12.3825-inch barrel and walnut grips and was configured to accommodate a removable wire stock. This pistol was built on a No. 2 Size frame (normally only used for .30 and .32 cal. Vest Pockets.
(Bob Hatfield Photo)

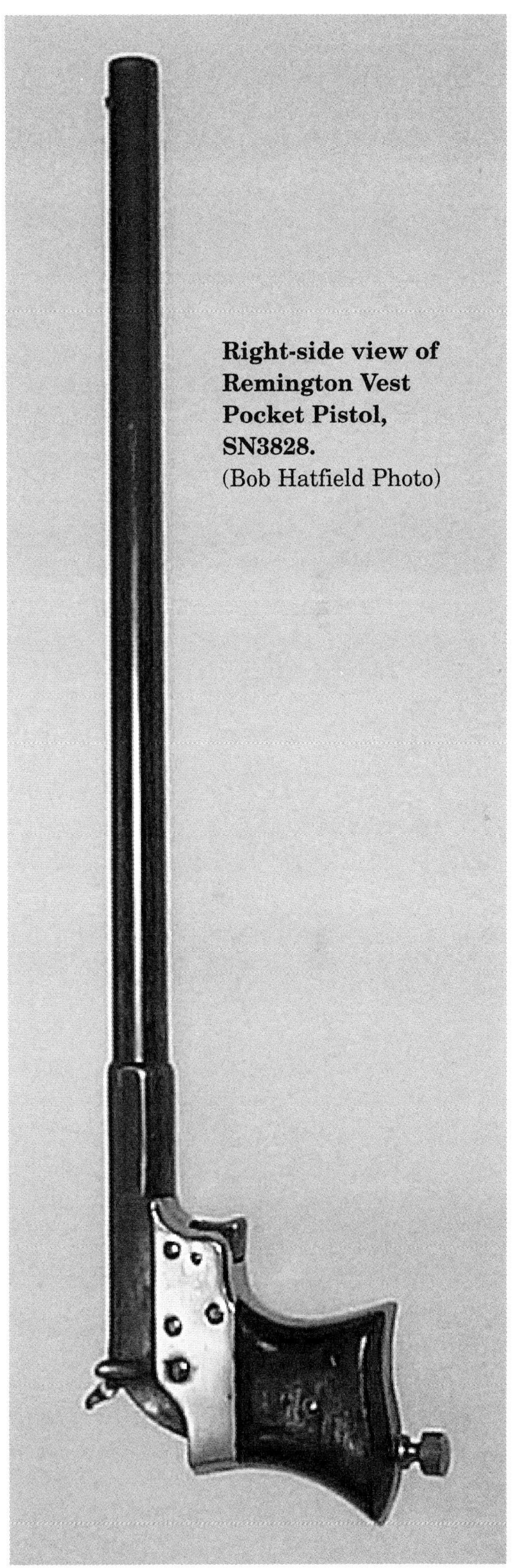

Right-side view of Remington Vest Pocket Pistol, SN3828.
(Bob Hatfield Photo)

The conclusion reached thus far:

Remington manufactured Vest Pocket Pistols in four calibers: .22 cal. (RF) short, .30 cal. (RF) short, .32 cal. (RF) short, and .41 cal. (RF) short

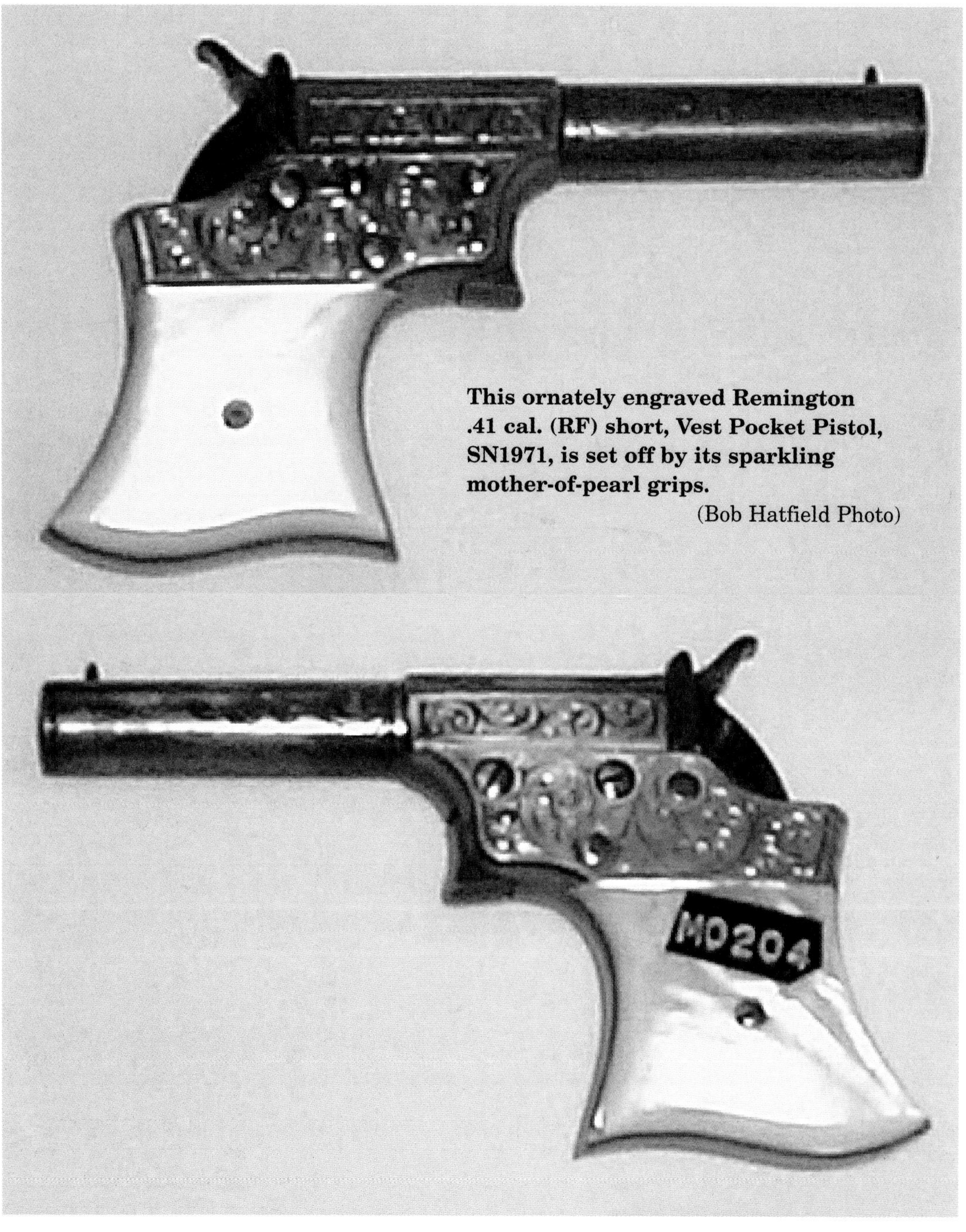

This ornately engraved Remington .41 cal. (RF) short, Vest Pocket Pistol, SN1971, is set off by its sparkling mother-of-pearl grips.
(Bob Hatfield Photo)

Chapter Five

During What Time Period Were They Made?

The estimated time span in which Remington manufactured Vest Pocket Pistols has been fairly well established as some time during or shortly after the Civil War through about 1888. There are, nevertheless, some differences of opinion. The views of others mentioned herein are offered with minimal editorial comment.

Hank Wieand Bowman (1953) suggested that production started in 1863. Bowman went on to relate that Remington continued production of these small single-shot pistols through 1867. That end date would indicate that Remington terminated manufacture eleven years before they quit advertising Vest Pocket Pistols for sale, at least the .22 caliber, No. 1 Size models. As mentioned and illustrated in Chapter One, Remington continued to advertise the .22 caliber models more than twenty years after 1867.

The October 1, 1861, patent date of William H. Elliot's Patent Number 33,382 can be found on the top of the barrel/receivers of all of the marked Remington Vest Pocket Pistols. Remington Vest Pocket Pistol serial number 1, which was produced in .22 caliber, had that patent information on the top of the barrel/receiver near the breech.

Patent information on the #1 pistol reads: (On two lines)

REMINGTON'S ILION N.Y.
PATENT OCT. 1, 1861

The majority of the large split-breech Remington Vest Pocket Pistols bear the patent date of Nov. 15, 1864, in addition to the Oct. 1, 1861, date. The barrel/receivers of these pistols have two lines of type, which read:

REMINGTON'S ILION N.Y.
PATD OCT. 1, 1861, NOV. 15, 1864

Remington Vest Pocket Pistol serial number 2 was manufactured in .30 caliber on a split-breech frame. Information on the Vest Pocket with serial number 2 submitted as part of this research did not report any barrel markings. The serial number was found on the toe of the frame, under the left grip. Without the telltale 1864 patent date to prove otherwise, this pistol could have been manufactured prior to issuance of that patent. (We have all seen products that were made before the Patent was issued, you know — "Patent Pending".)

Leon Wier based his estimated dates of manufacture, 1865 to at least 1888, on the fact that during the years 1861 into 1865, this country was involved in the Civil War.

Now, when you stop and think about that, doesn't it seem unlikely that one of the nation's major firearms manufacturers would be using even a small part of its production capacity to produce small single-shot pistols for the civilian market? All of this country's arms producers were strained to the maximum just to provide basic military long guns and handguns.

Wier contends that production of Remington Vest Pocket Pistols started in general in 1865, and the .22 caliber models were produced until at least 1888, with larger models being made until at least 1876 in .30, .32 and .41 calibers. His estimated dates were all subsequent to both patent dates.

Kirkland (1988), Flayderman (1994), Hatch (1956) and Schwing (1996) agreed that the inclusive 1865–1888 dates identified the period in which Remington manufactured their Vest Pocket Pistols. *The Standard Catalog of Firearms* (6th Edition) also depicted the inclusive dates of Remington Vest Pocket Pistol production as the period from 1865 to 1888. Robert W.D. Ball (1995) agreed with those dates of manufacture.

Roy Marcot (1998) advanced the theory that production of Remington Vest Pocket Pistols was introduced in .22 caliber sometime during the Civil War, but the larger split-breech models were not offered until 1866.

To further muddy the waters, a recent purchase of a .30 caliber Remington Vest Pocket Pistol prompted conjecture that there may be reason to conclude that at least both .22 caliber and .30 caliber Vest Pockets were manufactured as early as 1863.

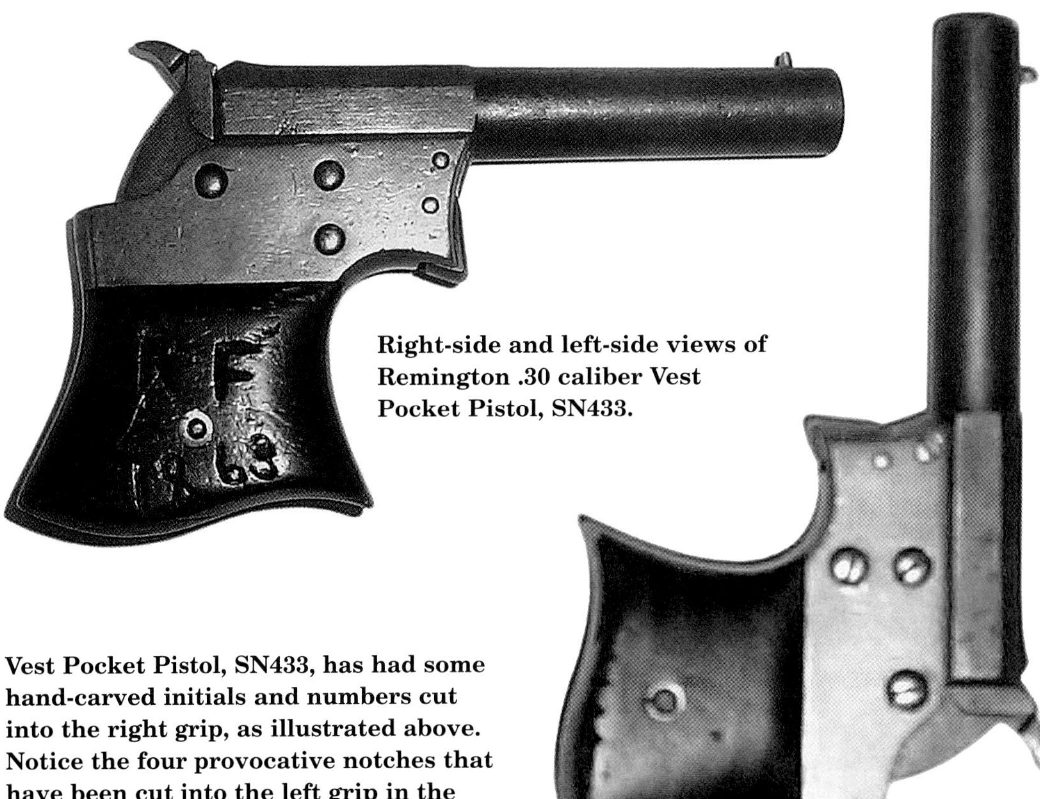

Right-side and left-side views of Remington .30 caliber Vest Pocket Pistol, SN433.

Vest Pocket Pistol, SN433, has had some hand-carved initials and numbers cut into the right grip, as illustrated above. Notice the four provocative notches that have been cut into the left grip in the illustration at the right, which is a left-side view of the same pistol.

Digress with me for a moment and just let your imagination go wild with this one. Just think about it. Can't you just visualize some stalwart citizen stepping out into the street and calling out the "Bad Guy" challenging him to stand up against the ferocity of our hero's .30 caliber Remington Vest Pocket Pistol? After which our "Good Guy" would calmly carve another notch in the left grip of his trusty Vest Pocket Pistol.

Enough fantasy, let's venture back toward reality.

Deeply carved in the right walnut grip above the grip screw are the two initials "R" and "F", and below the grip screw is carved the date "1863". Let's assume that the initials and the date were carved in 1863. That would indicate that at least 433 Remington Vest Pocket Pistols had been manufactured prior to the end of 1863. (We will probably never find out to whom the initials "R" and "F" referred.)

Remington Vest Pocket Pistols were put into production during the Civil War in 1863. Based on Remington advertising, .22 caliber Vest Pocket Pistol production continued until at least 1888. Production of the No. 2 Size, .30 and .32 caliber, as well as the No. 3 Size in .41 caliber models was carried out about the same time and continued until they were phased out somewhat earlier than the No. 1 Size was.

Armed with this information and continuing in the same direction, one could assume that production of .32 caliber and .41 caliber models began during the period, as well.

Our survey contains twenty-eight .22 caliber Vest Pocket samples, another twenty-three .30 caliber models, and another seven in .32 caliber, plus twelve .41 caliber models, all with serial numbers under 433. Are we to conclude that Remington built at least 433 Vest Pocket Pistols prior to the end of 1863? Of course not!

Talk about fiction!

Remington would have been manufacturing split-breech Vest Pocket models prior to the November 15, 1864, patent date. There is no way they could have known about that 1864 date. Before we can get very excited about this, we must realize that the Vest Pocket Pistol with the serial number 3 was also made in .30 caliber and was marked with the November 15, 1864, patent date (along with the Oct. 1, 1861, date that we have found on the .22 caliber models). So, sometime prior to November 15, 1864, Remington made two Vest Pocket Pistols.

Therefore, what really makes sense is the theory that production of Remington Vest Pocket Pistols in any real quantity did not occur until after cessation of the Civil War. Lee surrendered on Palm Sunday, April 9, 1865. The rebellion was quelled, providing the opportunity and the necessity for arms manufacturers to switch over to fast-selling products for the civilian market.

Remington, as one of those firearms producers, needed to court the civilian market to help insure its survival. Small personal defense weapons, such as the Remington Vest Pocket Pistols, were ideal products for that period of time. They would probably have been especially well suited for the "Carpet-Bagger" types, since they were small, flat and easily concealed.

The postwar period provided an excellent opportunity for proliferation of reasonably priced merchandise, such as Vest Pocket Pistols, to be offered to the general public. Such an action would have helped to keep production facilities operating. Thus, assisting Remington to retain more of its work force and possibly increase their market share.

Easterners were more apt to purchase the smaller size .22 caliber Vest Pocket Pistol. Eastern fashions, men's in particular, tended to be somewhat more form-fitting than the attire worn in the West. Expand that thought and it becomes quite logical that the larger caliber Vest Pocket Pistols would have been more acceptable to people in the West. This thought is borne out by the availability of Remington Vest Pocket Pistols at contemporary gun shows. You see more of the smaller size Vest Pocket Pistols at eastern U.S. gun shows while seeing more of the larger split-breech models at gun shows in the West.

Remington advertising flyers and catalogs indicate that production of .22 caliber, No. 1 Size, Vest Pocket Pistols continued through 1888. The larger split-breech models were phased out during the late 1870s.

CONCLUSION —

Remington started to produce .22 caliber Vest Pocket Pistols prior to the end of 1863, and production of No. 1 Size, .22 caliber models continued through 1888. The larger split-breech models were produced in .30, .32 and .41 calibers. Production commenced sometime subsequent to the November 15, 1864, patent date, and they were phased out during the late 1870s.

Chapter Six

What Were Their Specifications? What Markings Were Revealed?

The markings reportedly found on .22 caliber Remington Vest Pocket Pistols include these identifying markings which appear on the top of the receiver. In the majority of cases they read from the muzzle to the breech.

REMINGTON'S ILION. N.Y.
PATENT OCT. 1, 1861

Take a close look at the exploded views and the parts lists for the three different sizes of Remington Vest Pocket Pistols. *(You will find them in Appendices 5A, 6A and 7A).*

The No. 1 Size models were made in .22 caliber rimfire short only. These were the smallest of the Remington Vest Pocket Pistols. In this model only, the hammer also serves as the breech block. Another distinctive feature of the .22 caliber, No. 1 Size, Vest Pocket Pistol is the absence of an extractor. Close observation reveals two small scallops at the rear of the barrel/receiver on either side of the chamber.

With a .22 caliber, rimfire short cartridge loaded in the chamber, these notches allow the thumbnail and the nail of the forefinger to simply grasp the rim of the cartridge case. Removal of the expended cartridge case or of a loaded cartridge requires very little effort, and is readily accomplished by pulling the cartridge straight back.

The upper frame is an integral part of the No. 1 Size Vest Pocket Pistol's barrel/receiver. A separate frame component, which fastens to the barrel/receiver, accommodates the grips. (Which, incidentally, were available in walnut, rosewood, pearl and ivory). This lower frame also houses the main spring.

The entire .22 caliber, rimfire short model consists of only sixteen parts. Looking for a parts list led me to the Remington's 1877 catalog. (The truth of the matter is that, without the assistance of Leon Wier and Jay Huber, I could still be searching for a parts list.) Be certain to really check out the title of the publication, shown on page 58.

Now take another look! — "Illustrated, Remingtons' Breech-Loading Rifles, Shot Guns, Revolvers, Repeaters and Ammunition, Gun Mounting, &c., 1877." *(Catalog)*

The subtle notches on each side of the chamber have been slightly exaggerated to facilitate easier recognition.

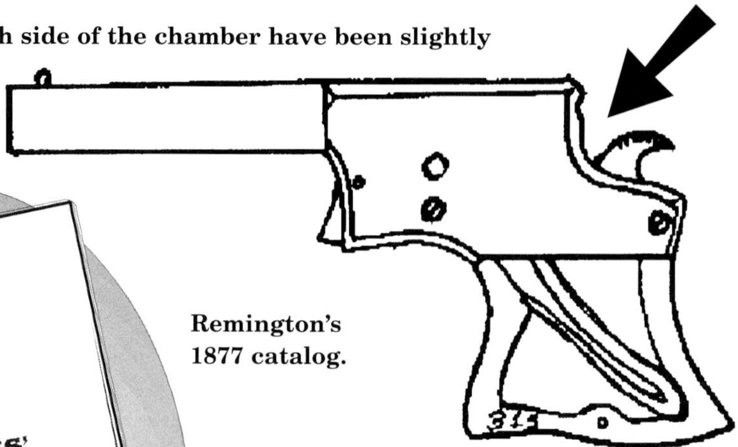

ILLUSTRATED
REMINGTONS'
BREECH-LOADING
Rifles, Shot Guns, Revolvers,
Repeaters and Ammunition,
Gun Mounting, &c.
1877.

Remington's 1877 catalog.

Please note that nowhere in that expansive yet impressive title are you able to find the terms: "Single Shot," "Vest Pocket" or "Pistol." Inside this catalog, you will not find reference to any size Vest Pocket Pistol other than the No. 1 Size, .22 caliber.

Was this an indication that manufacture of the No. 2 Size .30 caliber and .32 caliber models as well as the .41 caliber Vest Pocket Pistols had ceased by 1877?

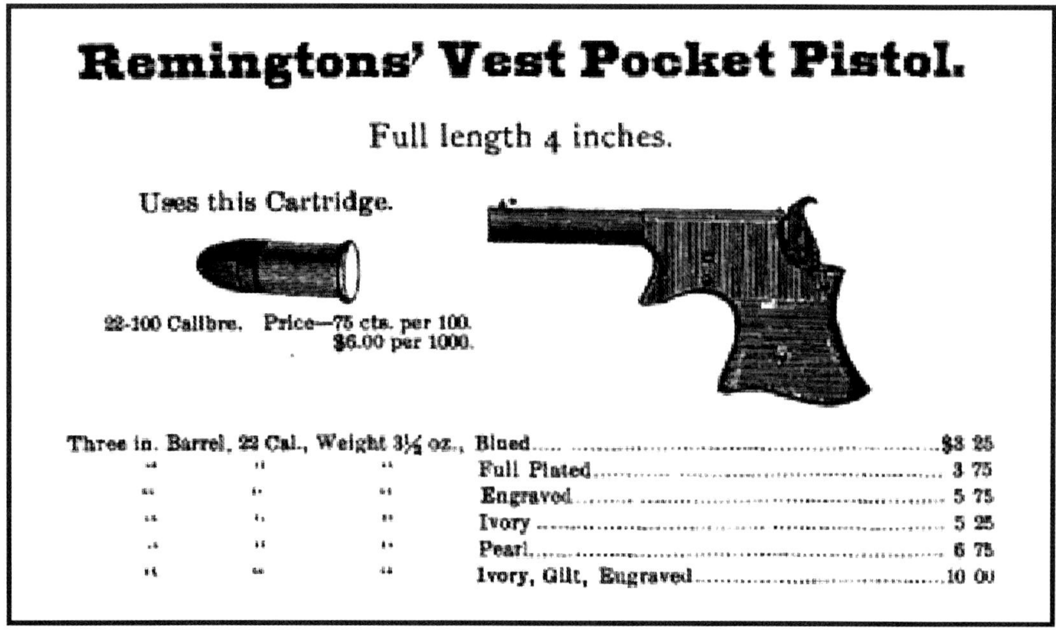

Remingtons' Vest Pocket Pistol.

Full length 4 inches.

Uses this Cartridge.

22-100 Calibre. Price—75 cts. per 100. $6.00 per 1000.

Three in. Barrel, 22 Cal., Weight 3½ oz.,	Blued	$3 25
" " "	Full Plated	3 75
" " "	Engraved	5 75
" " "	Ivory	5 25
" " "	Pearl	6 75
" " "	Ivory, Gilt, Engraved	10 00

Reprint of page 34 from the 1877 Remington catalog.

COMPONENT PARTS

OF

PISTOLS.

	N. M. Army.	Army.	Navy.	Belt.	Police.	New Pocket.	D. A. Pocket.	Smoot No. 1.	Rider Magazine.	Repeating.	D'ble Derringer	Derringer.	V. P. 1-22.
Arm, Carrier	$	$	$	$	$	$	$	$	$ 50	$	$	$	$
Barrel	2 12	1 75	1 50	1 50	1 37	1 25	75	3 00	1 50	2 00	2 25	75	1 75
Breech									75				
Bolt										25			
Bolt, Carrier								25					
Bolt, Stop	30	30	30	30	30	23		20					
Bolt, Locking											35		
Carrier									60				
Cylinder and Cones		2 60	2 25	2 25	2 00	1 87	1 50	2 00					
" Cartridge	3 00	3 00		2 25	2 25	2 00	2 00	2 00					
Cap, Magazine Tube									12				
Cones		10	10	10	10	10	10	10		35			
Escutcheon	10	10	10	10	10	10	10	10		10	10	10	10
Extractor	50							35					
Frame	3 50	3 00	2 75	2 75	2 50	2 25	2 25		2 00	2 50	2 35	1 15	75
Guard	60	50	50	50	50	40	25	1 00					
Gâte	50												
Hammers	62	62	62	62	60	50	46	50	60	45	60	60	45
Lever		1 00	95	95	90	75				15			
Moulds		75	75	75	75	50	50						
Pawl	25	20	20	20	20	25	25	20	25				
" Driver					10								
" Revolving										15			
" Cocking, Spring										35			
Plunger									08				

39

COMPONENT PARTS OF PISTOLS.

[CONTINUED]

	N. M. Army.	Army.	Navy.	Belt.	Police.	New Pocket.	D. A. Pocket.	Smoot, No. 1.	Rider Magaz'e	Repeating.	Db'l Derringer	Derringer.	V. P.—1-22.
Pin, Hammer	$	$	$	$	$	$	$ 08	$	$	$	$	$ 08	$
" Tip and Gate	02												
" Firing									08	15	25		
" Cocking							02						
" Center	40	40	35	35	35	26	26	40					
Plate Breech								50		25			
Ratchet											25		
Swivel and Ring	25												
Screws	02	02	02	02	02	02	02	02	02	02	02	02	02
Stock	60	50	50	50	50	40	60	56	50	50	50	50	35
Sear									16				
Stay										06			
Starter and Wiper							15						
Screw Driver and Wrench		18	18	18	18	18							
Stirrup D. A.	10			15			15		15	20	15		
Sight, Barrel		06	06	06	06	05							
Stud, Barrel		10	10	10	10	06							
Spring, Mag. Coiled	25								15				
" Main		25	20	20	20	15	20	30	35	20	30	10	15
" Sear	06								12				
" Trig. and Bolt	12	06	06	06	05	05			16		20	08	
" Extractor								15		15	15		
" Firing Pin											15		
" Carrier									12				
" Ratchet											20		
" Pawl								10					
Trigger	25	25	25	25	25	20	25	25	30	35	40	25	20
Tumbler, D. A.				35			35						
Tube, Magazine									25				
Tip	75												
Washer. Swivel and Ring	02												

40

Nonetheless, there is a listing of the component parts for the No. 1 Size, which were available at that time. Even though the quoted prices are extremely low by today's standards, when you add in two escutcheons, three screws and two grips (stocks), the total parts bill would be the staggering sum of $4.26. A visit to page 34 of the same catalog will reveal that a complete .22 caliber Remington Vest Pocket Pistol was available for only $3.25.

Plated, it would have cost $3.75. Engraved, $5.75. Ivory grips were $5.25. Pearl grips cost $6.75. (The works: Ivory, gilt and engraved went for a $10.00 bill, and for that period of time, a double sawbuck was a considerable amount of money).

THE 1877 CATALOG LISTED THESE COMPONENT PARTS FOR THE "V.P. 1–22"

(on pages 39 and 40)

Part	Cost
Barrel	$1.75
Escutcheon	.10
Frame	.75
Hammer	.45
Screws	.02
Stock	.35
Spring (main)	.15
Trigger	.20

The front sight post/pin was not listed as available. The hammer pin and the trigger retaining pin were not even included. The tiny coil trigger spring doesn't appear in the 1877 catalog listing either.

Doesn't it seem strange that the smallest parts were omitted from this catalog? The smaller the part, the easier it is to lose. The miniscule coil trigger spring is probably not subject to easy breakage, but being only about 3/16 of an inch long, it could sure disappear. Especially if it were to be accidentally dropped on the floor, and it wouldn't matter if that floor were dirt, carpet or whatever.

Under the heading "COMPONENT PARTS OF PISTOLS," located on pages 39 and 40 of the 1877 catalog, you will find that the column to the right is labeled:

"V. P. 1–22."

Four of the component parts of the .22 caliber Vest Pocket Pistol are listed on page 39, and another four available parts are to be found on page 40.

Since disassembly and assembly procedures are so obvious, even to the casual observer, I hesitated to include them. If you feel the urge to take one of these small pistols apart, take a look at the information contained in Appendix 8A.

***Curiosity has totally done in any number of the feline family.
When you have an old collectible firearm
and it is in reasonably decent condition, keep it clean.
Show it off and don't mess with it!***

Hesitate before you attempt to become an instant gunsmith. As simple as the directions may appear, especially the disassembly phase, there are times that the reassembly portion (that "just reverse the procedure" part of the process) occasionally is just a wee bit more demanding than the directions would lead you to believe.

Barrel markings found on the No. 2 Size and No. 3 Size models differ from those on the No. 1 Size. Remington, larger split-breech Vest Pocket Pistols not only have the Oct. 1, 1861, patent date, but the Nov. 15, 1864, patent date has been added.

The markings, found on the flat surface on top of the barrel/receiver of the larger models, read:

REMINGTON'S ILION. N.Y.
PATD OCT. 1. 1861. NOV. 15. 1864

Most responses to the surveys specified that the markings on the top of the barrel/receiver (on the receiver end) read from the muzzle to the breech. Only one reported markings reading from the breech to the muzzle. There were only two respondents who indicated their Vest Pocket Pistols had no barrel markings at all.

The No. 2 Size was manufactured in .30 caliber, rimfire short and in .32 caliber, rimfire short. (Only the No. 2 Size Vest Pocket Pistol was manufactured in more than one caliber.) The No. 3 Size was made in .41 caliber, rimfire short only. The overall style of the larger split-breech differs from the No. 1 Size Vest Pockets. The hammer does not serve as the breech block. This was the Remington introduction of the split breech in pistols.

Both of the larger sizes have split breeches with a drum-shaped hole that receives a retaining pin. On the cylindrical breech extension is a miniature post sticking out toward the chamber. This extension serves as an extractor.

When the split breech is pulled to the rear and arced down, the arc motion allows this extension to engage the cartridge case rim, pulling it to the rear, dislodging the spent cartridge case or loaded cartridge from the chamber.

Triggers in each of the larger sizes have extensions on the top-rear, which fit into the notches on the forward portions of the hammers.

The No. 3 Size, .41 caliber Remington Vest Pocket Pistol, serial number 958, incorporates a bent wire spring. The hook, illustrated on the left of the spring, fits around the trigger pin. The arc-shaped rear of the spring (the right end of the illustration is cradled in the curved section, on the upper forward surface of the hammer). The rear end of the spring fits against the split-breech to provide tension for smooth operation.

For some reason or other, the No. 3 Size, .41 caliber Remington Vest Pocket Pistol, serial number 2260, does *not* contain such a bent spring. This particular pistol has a part that is mounted on the hammer pin to the right of the hammer.

Its apparent purpose, like that of the bent wire spring in the Vest Pocket with the 958 serial number, is to ease opening and closing of the split breech. All other parts of these two .41 Caliber Vest Pocket Pistols are virtually interchangeable. Similar split-breech springs have not been found in No. 1 Size nor in No. 2 Size Vest Pockets Pistols.

Another idiosyncrasy evidenced by close scrutiny of the .41 caliber Vest Pocket Pistol is the placement of the number "32" in two locations: on the bottom side of the receiver close to the barrel, and again on the left side of the grip frame near the rear (behind the grip retaining pin extension). The most logical explanation is that they are assembly numbers. The different split-breech spring configurations and the addition of assembly numbers are, most likely, product improvements or changes made in the manufacturing process between the time of the earlier (958) serial number and the production of the later (2260) serial number.

When you compare the No. 2 Size with the No. 3 Size, you find that they both employ barrel/receiver extensions on the bottom side, which fit into their frames. Close inspection reveals that the No. 2 Size barrel/receiver extension is scalloped on the bottom.

The frames of the No. 2 Size .30 caliber and the .32 caliber models are interchangeable. (Please consider the fact that these little pistols were virtually handmade and would require some degree

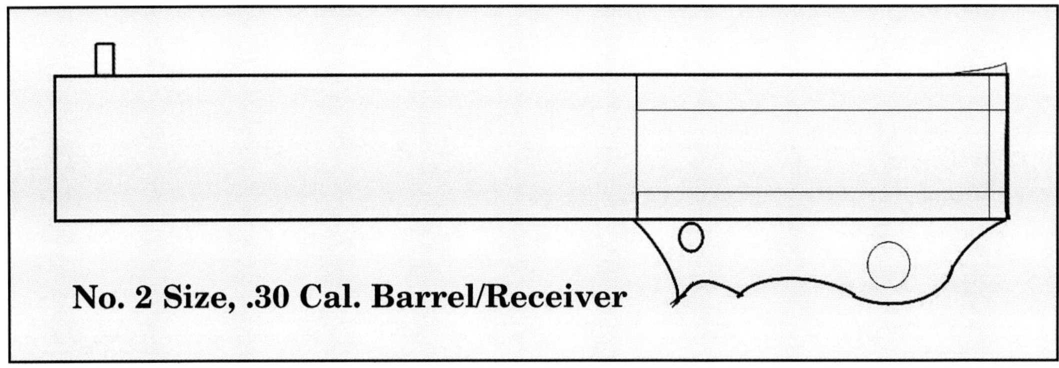

This illustration reveals the general shape of a .30 caliber (RF short) Vest Pocket Pistol barrel/receiver and the scalloped extension on the bottom of it that fits into the pistol frame.

of hand-fitting.) Other than minor fitting to accommodate the grip stabilizing pins, the No. 2 Size grips are interchangeable, also.

They utilize the same-sized main spring and the same-sized split breech. They share common sized triggers and identical hammers.

The tiny trigger spring will fit either the .30 or the .32 Remington Vest Pocket Pistols. Both of these caliber models were put together with screws and pins of the same size. The barrels, of

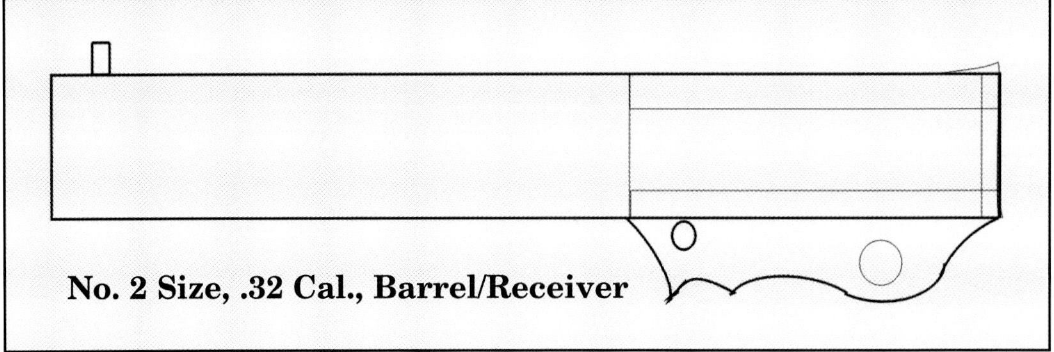

This illustration reveals the general shape of a .32 caliber (RF short) Vest Pocket Pistol barrel/receiver and the scalloped extension on the bottom of it that fits into the pistol frame. The extension is the same as the extension on the .30 caliber model.

course, are necessarily different to accommodate the two different calibers that were manufactured on the No. 2 Size frame.

Brass frames constituted about one-third of all the .30 caliber Vest Pockets encountered during the survey. Only .30 caliber Vest Pocket Pistols were reported as having had brass frames. Of the forty-two .30 caliber Vest Pocket Pistols included in this study, thirteen of them had been reported as having been produced with brass frames. Five were reported with iron frames. One No. 2 Size Vest Pocket Pistol was reported to have had a bronze frame. The remainder of the submissions failed to reveal what frame material was used.

The lower portion of the No. 3 Size, .41 caliber, barrel/receiver extension is parallel to the lower edge of the receiver.

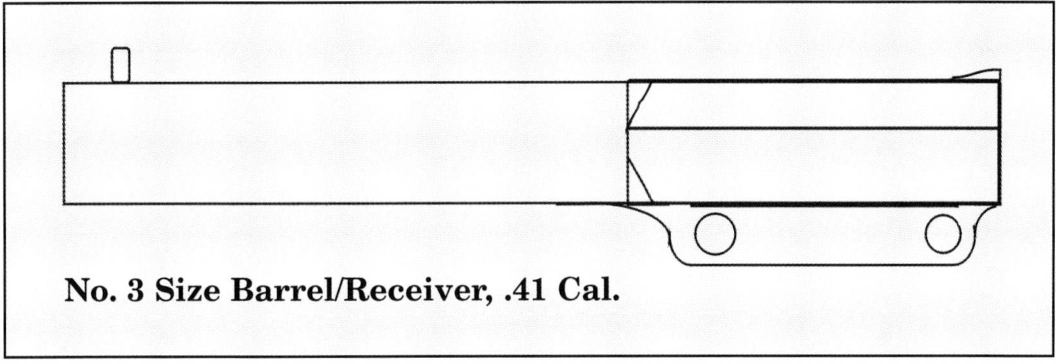

No. 3 Size Barrel/Receiver, .41 Cal.

Compare the extension on the bottom of this barrel/receiver with the scalloped extension on the No. 2 Size Vest Pocket Pistols in the illustrations on page 62.

Minor elements appear to have been custom-made. After all, Remington Vest Pocket Pistols were hand finished. There would certainly be some inconsequential appearance differences.

The checkering on the hammers, for example, as well as on the split-breech top surfaces of the larger model Vest Pocket Pistols, was not done in one set pattern. The following illustrations of various patterns found on randomly selected models have been enlarged here and on page 64 to emphasize the checkering.

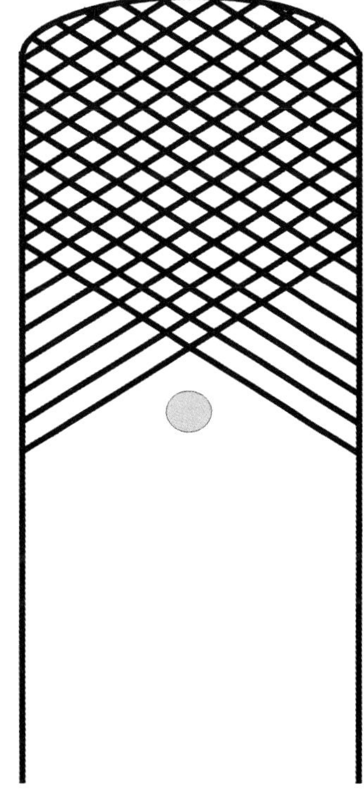

Hammer Checkering, No. 1 Size Remington Vest Pocket Pistol, .22 Caliber RF Short, SN10178.
(enlarged to illustrate checkering detail

Remington No. 2 and No. 3 Size Vest Pocket Pistols

Hammer and Split-Breech Checkering

(enlarged to illustrate checkering detail)

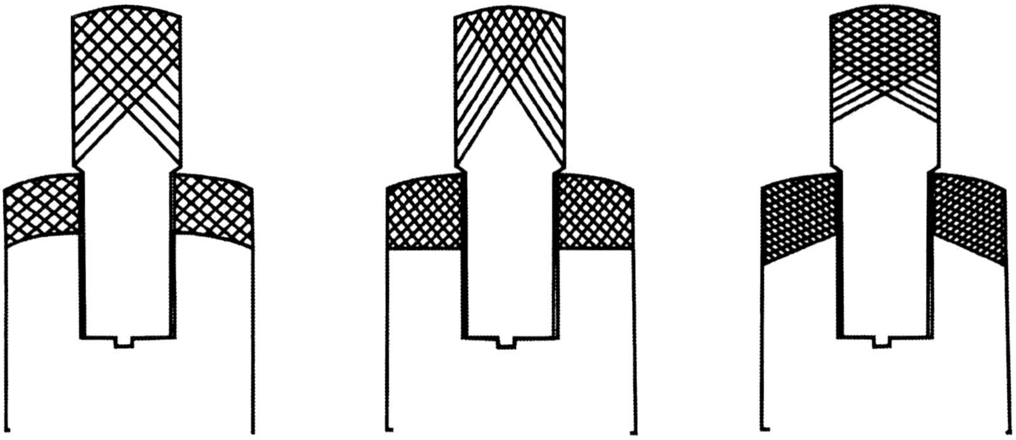

Remington .30 Caliber RF Short Vest Pocket Pistol SN1540	Remington .32 Caliber RF Short Vest Pocket Pistol SN191	Remington .41 Caliber RF Short Vest Pocket Pistol SN2260

Chapter Seven

Were Vest Pocket Wire-Stocked Buggy/Bicycle Rifles Made by Remington?

In spite of whether or not Remington actually manufactured long-barreled, wire-stocked rifles using any or all of their basic No. 1, No. 2 or No. 3 Size Vest Pocket Pistol frames, the dilemma of just what to call the existing specimens remains. They can be found in any number of publications referred to as Remington... "Vest Pocket Wire Stocked Rifles," "Wire Stocked Rifles," "Wire Stocked Buggy Rifles," "Vest Pocket Buggy Rifles," "Pocket Bicycle Rifles," and/or "Folding Stock Pocket Rifles."

Take a look at the interesting display of so-called "Remington Buggy Rifles" that appears in *Deringer in America, Volume II.* [Eberhart/Wilson ('93)]. A very limited number were reported in the survey information for this book, which includes those in R.L. Wilson/Doug Eberhart research.

Eberhart believes that the "Wire Stock Buggy Rifles" were made by Remington. He thinks that they resulted from special orders from individual customers. This could help explain the differences of barrel lengths, variety of finishes, the design/configuration of the wire stocks, the sight selection and the methods of mounting the sights.

The wire-stocked pocket/buggy/bicycle rifle barrels/frames were marked, in many instances, with both the 1861 and 1864 patent numbers, as were the larger caliber Remington Vest Pocket Pistols. This could have contributed to the belief that these "wire-stocked pocket/buggy/bicycle rifles" were all complete products of Remington.

There is still much to be learned about these long-barreled varieties, especially those that were manufactured in .32 caliber and in .41 caliber. Additional research is going to be required.

In a field of just thirteen samples reported during this study, eleven different barrel lengths were submitted/encountered. (This sure doesn't indicate that these special configurations were manufactured with the thought of any of them occupying a regular position in the Remington product line.) The various barrel lengths uncovered in this research were:

7.5 inches	16.25 inches
9 inches	16.375 inches
10 inches	13.875 inches*
15.5 inches	18 inches
16 inches	22.5 inches
16.75 inches	

**(The barrel of the 13.875-inch specimen is marked "Wighlman's Approved".)*

Robert D. Ball ('95) contends the "Buggy Rifles" are products of one or more very talented expert gunsmiths who built them using Remington Vest Pocket Pistol frames. The illustrations in Ball's **Golden Age of Collecting** *do not reveal the serial numbers of the two "Buggy Rifles" shown. They do appear to be the same two guns that were featured in the Moldenhauer Collection Auction presentation. Their serial numbers were not identified in that publication either. Because of the different barrel lengths and other descriptive information, these two examples were not the same as any of the other specimens included in this study. That is, not until Elliott L. Burka sent me a wealth of information and photographs. One of the Remington Long Barrel Pocket Rifles shown in the aforementioned publications is illustrated in these two original Elliott L. Burka photos. Even though some were reported with standard Remington markings on the top of the frame, others were described as having different barrel markings and numbers. Barrels on some were reported to have had rifled sleeves inserted in the barrels of the original Remington factory barrel/frame.*

(Elliott L. Burka Photos)

Right-side view of "Remington" Pocket rifle, SN2782, Assembly #213, blue and nickel.

View of left side of the same Pocket Rifle with folding stock, 15½-inch barrel and rosewood grips.

Were Vest Pocket Wire-Stocked Buggy/Bicycle Rifles Made by Remington?

Elliott Burka, the owner of this wire-stocked Remington Vest Pocket Pistol, is thoroughly convinced that this particular "Pocket Rifle" was produced by Remington, but did not offer any suggestion as to what that inscription might signify. The same collector asserts that one piece in his "Remington Vest Pocket/Buggy/Bicycle Rifle" collection was manufactured especially to be displayed at the 1876 Centennial celebration in Philadelphia.

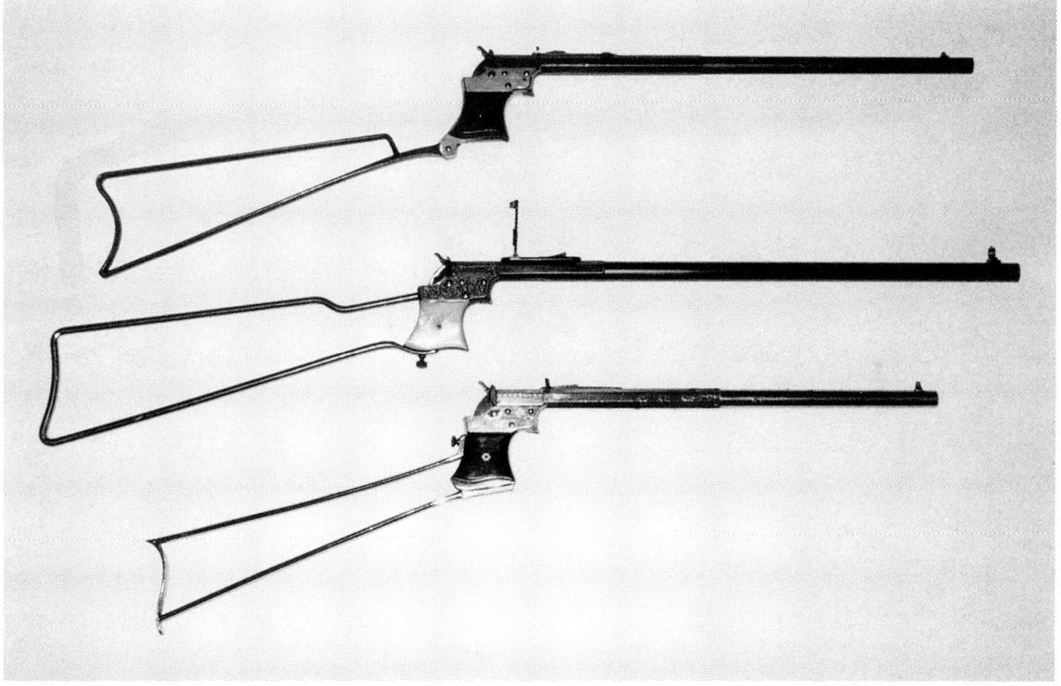

Three exotic Long-Barreled Pocket Rifles. (Elliott L. Burka Collection)

As Jim Shaffer so aptly put it:

"There are no absolutes in gun research!"

That seems to certainly fit in right here, doesn't it?

Answers to the following questions would certainly be very helpful in solving the "Remington Vest Pocket Wire-stocked/Buggy/Bicycle Rifle" quandary:

First of all —

- Were they really built by Remington? Some of them? All of them? Any of them?
- Were the wire stocks, stationary as well as folding models, products of Remington?
- Were the stocks built by an outside provider for Remington?
- Couldn't they, or at least some of the surviving samples, have been products of some very capable gunsmiths using Remington Vest Pocket Pistol frames?

Both of these speculative theories tend to be reinforced by the limited, existing information: (1) The buggy rifles were built by Remington, *and* (2) They are products of expert artisans using Remington Vest Pocket Pistol frames.

- Close scrutiny of available photographs and illustrations reveals significant design inconsistencies, such as the differing shapes of the wire stocks *and* the fact that some of the wire skeleton stocks fold, while others don't.
- The manner in which the stocks attach to the frames differ. Even the knurled knobs used to attach the wire stock to the frame are not alike, and some wire stocks appear quite amateurishly

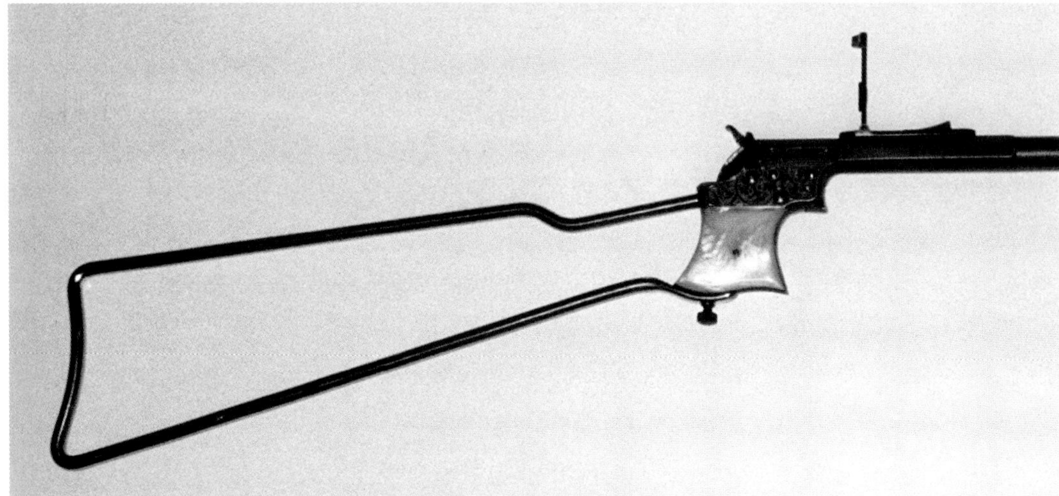

Notice the manner in which the stocks are fastened to the respective frames. This one, for example, is connected behind the frame and again to the bottom of the frame, and it does not fold! (Elliott L. Burka Photo)

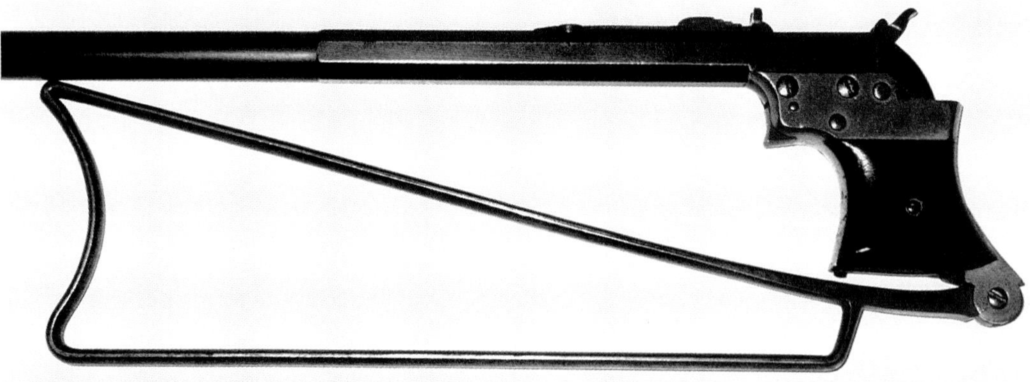

By comparison, check the manner in which this wire stock connects to the frame. Totally different from the other sample shown. This stock fits on a hinge pin and folds forward under the frame and the barrel. Also, please note that there is no knurled knob to secure it to the frame. (Elliott L. Burka Photo)

constructed. One explanation for this could very well be that they were homemade replacements for misplaced or lost original stocks.

- Some have rifled barrel sleeves that were made to fit into original "factory barrels/frames," some don't.
- Sights vary from weapon to weapon.
- Location of front and rear sights vary.
- Barrel lengths vary considerably.
- No two wire-stocked Remington Vest Pocket Pistols encountered are alike.

When you pause to really ponder these circumstances, even more questions are generated: 1) If these unique configurations are truly products resulting from "Special Order" requests from individual customers, why aren't there any of the "Fancy Nature" characteristics usually associated with "One-of-kind," custom-made firearms? 2) Where are the engraved models?

When Elliott Burka was asked these questions, he supplied photographs of this splendid plated and engraved pocket rifle with a wire stock. These photographs certainly disprove any thought that custom, presentation-grade Pocket/Buggy/Wire-stock rifles had not been manufactured. However, to be able to prove that any of them had been manufactured by Remington is another task in itself. Questions that come to mind when these unique weapons are scrutinized, include:

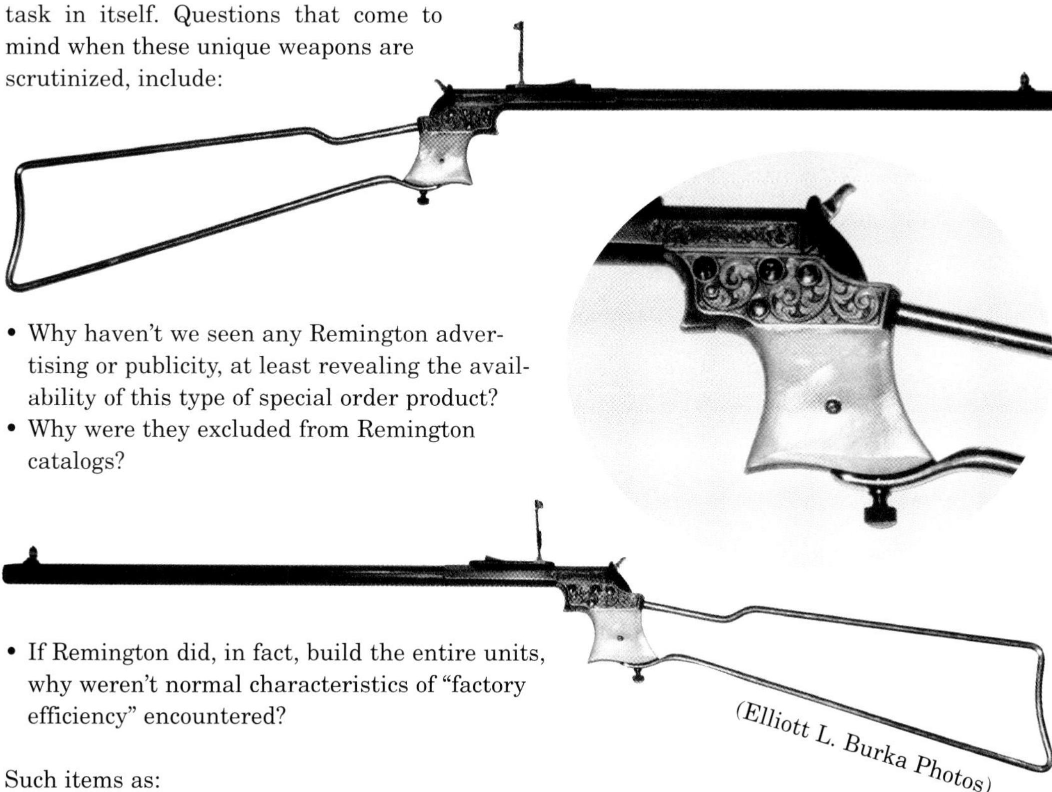

(Elliott L. Burka Photos)

- Why haven't we seen any Remington advertising or publicity, at least revealing the availability of this type of special order product?
- Why were they excluded from Remington catalogs?

- If Remington did, in fact, build the entire units, why weren't normal characteristics of "factory efficiency" encountered?

Such items as:

- "Standardized" folding and/or regular rigid wire stocks?
- Consistent placement of the knurled stock retaining knobs?

When you take a close look at illustrations of a group of individual long-barreled Pocket/Buggy/Bicycle/Wire-stocked rifles, their idiosyncracies are easier to discern. Compare sights and their placement. Pay particular attention to the manner in which the wire-stocks are fitted to each of them.

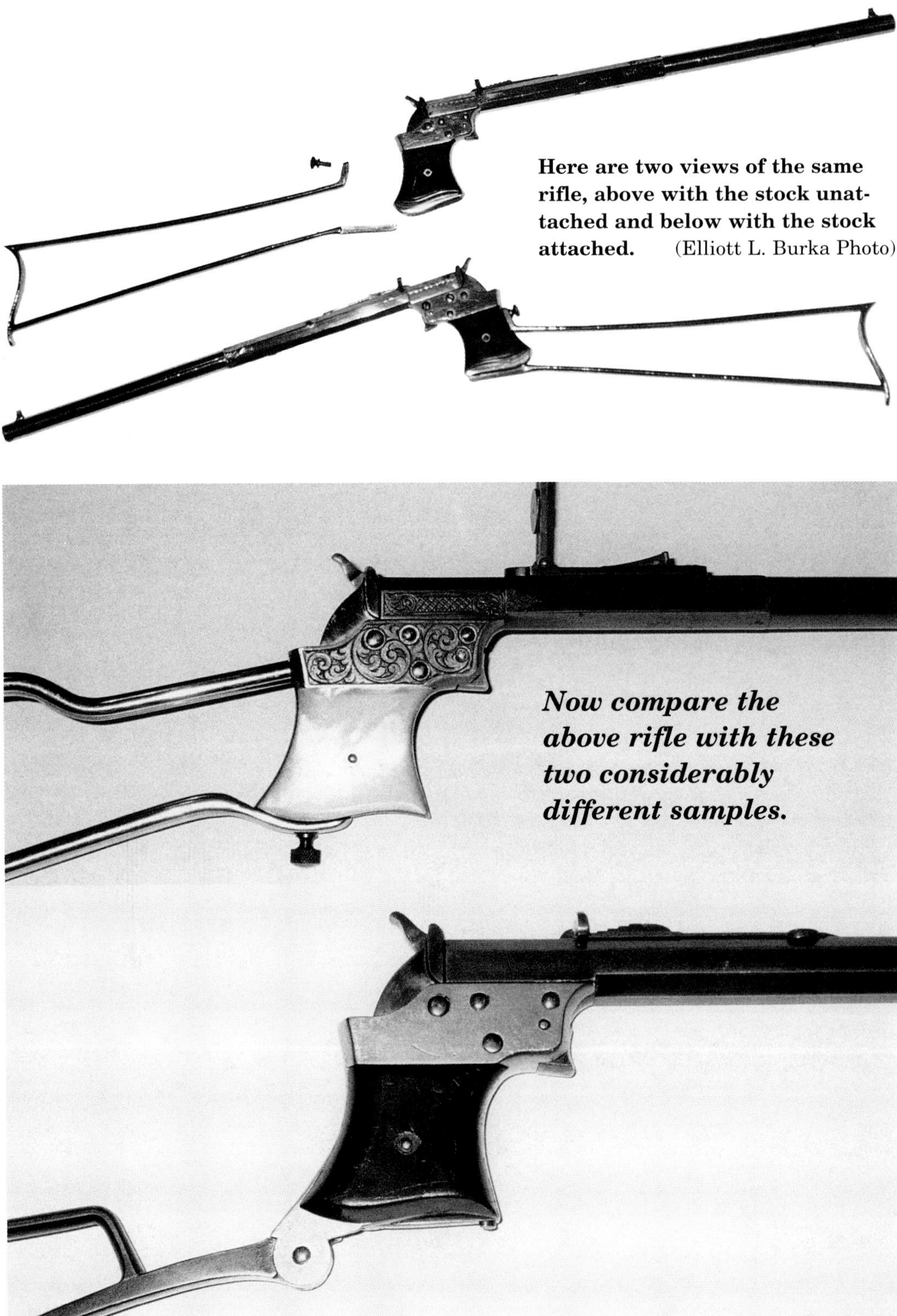

Here are two views of the same rifle, above with the stock unattached and below with the stock attached. (Elliott L. Burka Photo)

Now compare the above rifle with these two considerably different samples.

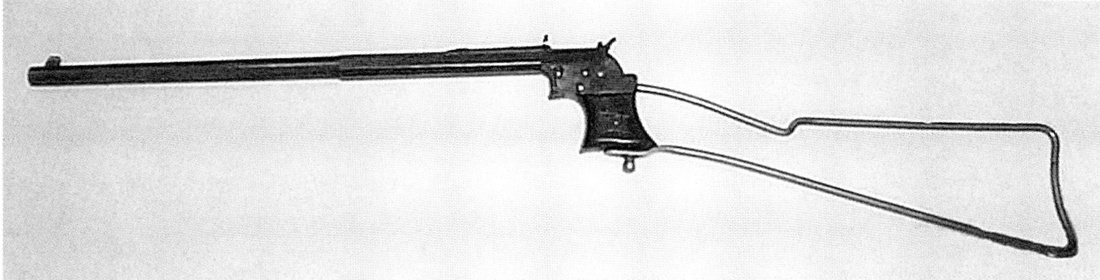

One of the "'Buggy Rifles" on display at the Remington Arms Museum in Ilion, New York.
(Elliott L. Burka Photo)

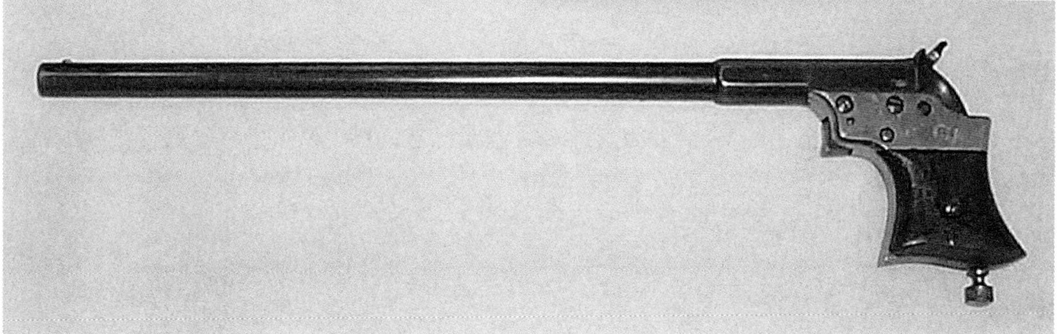

A shorter barrel model in Remington's Museum. (Elliott L. Burka Photo)

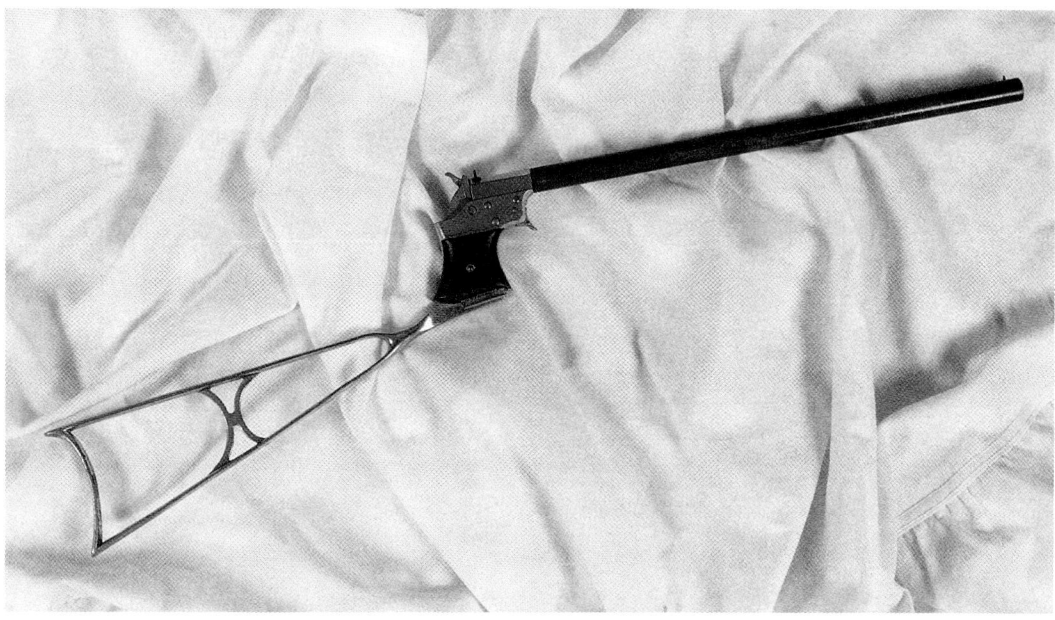

Remington Vest Pocket Buggy Rifle, SN2723, .22 caliber, removable stock. Built on (.41 caliber type) No. 3 Size frame.
(RSA member Larry Moody Collection. Photo by Drew Moody)

Perhaps there is an old Remington advertisement, or maybe a piece of factory paperwork not yet revealed in someone's collection, which will surface to help solve some of the unanswered questions. Even with firsthand inspection, it would be difficult, if not impossible, to determine for certain if Remington did actually build these unique pieces on a special-order basis.

Among the firearms in the Remington Firearms Museum in Ilion, New York, are two long-barreled Vest Pockets built on No. 2 Remington Vest Pocket frames. They are fitted with .22 caliber barrels of different lengths. The barrel of one of these "buggy rifle" configuration's measures 15.25 inches and the other is 12.3825 inches long. The knobs on the bottom of the grip frame are quite different. Note in these pictures that the weapon with the removable wire stock has a retaining knob that is virtually round and has been drilled through. Actually, it has the appearance of a lanyard swivel. The other model with the shorter barrel has a knurled knob. Compare the sights. The shorter-barreled model has no rear sight other than a groove in the rear of the receiver. The stocked model has an adjustable rear sight. Even the front sights are different. Another dissimilarity is the barrel design.

Any evidence that these two "Buggy Rifles" were complete products of Remington has proven to be very elusive. If Remington did have a hand in the making of any of the "Buggy Rifles," other than the basic Vest Pocket Pistol or even just the frame, they probably built them as prototypes, possibly for special occasions, e.g., Centennial recognition, or some other special occasion. These firearms must not have been approved for manufacture as a regular component of the Remington line. Surveying what has been uncovered up until now, I must conclude:

Though it appears that Remington did assemble some Long-Barreled Pocket/Buggy/Bicycle/Wire-Stocked Rifles for very special occasions, they did not build any of them for the regular retail market.

Assumptions and Conclusions...

The proper name for any of these single-shot pistols is "Remington Vest Pocket Pistols," regardless of what size they are and in what caliber they were produced.

More survey samples must be found to reinforce verification of the "Single-Series" of serial numbers for all caliber Vest Pocket Pistols, inclusively. I must subscribe to the "Single Serial Number Series hypothesis," even though there is proof of one (only one) duplicated serial number. Perhaps a scheduler assigned the same number twice, in error, or maybe a worker stamped the wrong serial number. Without more examples of duplicated serial numbers, it is incomprehensible to believe that each Vest Pocket size had its own series of sequential serial numbers starting with number 1.

Remington manufactured Vest Pocket Pistols
in only four different calibers:

.22 caliber rimfire short
.30 caliber rimfire short
.32 caliber rimfire short
.41 caliber rimfire short

...using three size frames:

No. 1 Size (.22 caliber models)
No. 2 Size (.30 and .32 caliber models)
No. 3 Size (.41 caliber models)

Although there is a known prototype .38 caliber Remington Vest Pocket Pistol in existence, I do not believe that Remington built any for the retail trade. This was probably a pattern gun that was rejected as a product for manufacture.

Additionally, all-out efforts need to be exerted to help resolve unanswered questions concerning the Remington Vest Pocket Pistols. Collectors of those samples not already included herein are encouraged to participate in future research efforts. I heartily recommend that individuals possessing copies of Remington, distributor and/or dealer advertising that are not already generally known, share that information with other collectors. If you possess any such information, send a copy to the *RSA Journal* editor, Roy Marcot, so he may share it with all of us.

All gun advertisers, commercial and individual, must be encouraged by all of us to include the serial number of each and every gun used in all advertising. Publications must be encouraged to suggest to advertisers to include each weapon's serial number in all advertising, even if that additional portion were printed "Free of Charge."

Inserting "Serial #xxxx" or "No. xxxx" or "SN: xxxx" wouldn't take up much space, but it sure would be of great assistance to researchers. So when you advertise firearms for sale, please make the extra effort to include serial numbers and encourage others to do the same.

Auction companies need to be contacted to encourage them to donate a set of their past catalogs to The Remington Society of America, for research efforts, just as the Rock Island (IL)

Auction house and the Faintich Auction house in St. Louis have done. After all, the more collectors know about antique and collectible firearms, the more interest there will be and the bigger and better that market will be.

While subscribing to the separate series of serial numbers for each caliber (or size) Remington Vest Pocket Pistol theory, and considering all of the serial numbers in this effort (up to 84575, when confirmed), the total production number rises to about 85,000. Most known sources have guesstimated that about 25,000 were produced in .22 caliber (No. 1 Size), alone. A majority of those sources also concluded that an additional 10,000, more or less, were produced in .30 caliber and .32 caliber (No. 2 Size) along with the .41 caliber (No. 3 Size), inclusively. The 1997 monograph (relying on the separate serial number series for each caliber theory) suggested that total production could have topped 61,942, indicating that nearly 62,000 Remington Vest Pocket Pistols were manufactured. Assuming that our sampling is a true cross-section of production totals, about half of all Vest Pocket Pistols produced would have been .22 caliber on No. 1 Size frames, an additional 20% or so in the No. 2 Size (about 12% in .30 caliber and 8% in .32 caliber). That would leave about 28% of the total production in .41 caliber, No. 3 Size. The remaining 4% would be Long Barrel/Pocket/Buggy/Bicycle Rifles. And, of course, the "Publisher's Note" by Stuart Mowbray on page 42 suggests an entirely different interpretation.

I agree with Jim Shaffer that brass frames were used on some .30 caliber models. During this research effort, those brass frames have been encountered in only .30 caliber Remington Vest Pocket Pistols with serial numbers under 500.

My conclusions concerning the inclusive dates when Remington manufactured Vest Pocket Pistols are basically in line with most other sources. However, I do agree with Roy Marcot ('98) that production probably started sometime during the Civil War. Vest Pocket production started before the end of 1863 and then was accelerated in 1865 after the war ended. Since Remington was advertising Vest Pockets up until 1888, manufacture must have lasted at least that long. "The Single Series of Serial Numbers Hypothesis" indicates that production of the larger calibers probably ceased considerably before 1888. Based on known advertising and catalog samples, the manufacture of the No. 2 Size and No. 3 Size models probably ceased in the late 1870s.

I agree with Leon Wier's ('94) supposition: "It is highly unlikely that Remington employees secretly took unmarked Vest Pocket components out of the Ilion factory and built complete weapons at home."

How This Study Was Conducted

– *Research Techniques* –

You read earlier about all of the assistance received while putting this study together. Many of the items listed below resulted from suggestions from others. For the most part, the research techniques employed in this endeavor are simplistic, common-sense approaches. A former grade school teacher of mine once explained how the mainstream individual can stay abreast with those who seem to really know it all: "Forget the fables about it's not what you know, but whom you know. The real secret to knowledge is in the libraries of the world...it is just knowing where to find it...that helps you keep up with everyone else."

Space is being devoted here to point out the research techniques used, for two major reasons:

1. Perhaps there are others who have never done any research at all, let alone "Gun Research." If any of you would like to find out more about a particular gun or series of guns, I hope this will encourage you to undertake the search.
2. There are some who do this sort of thing on a regular basis. I am certain they utilize much more sophisticated methods than the steps outlined below. My purpose in listing the procedures used in this effort is to encourage them to share more of their secrets, shortcuts and tricks of the trade.

Here's how this effort was accomplished (Also included are some suggestions on how the procedure could or should have been improved):

- A concise, specialized research survey form was devised. It was later improved based on numerous suggestions volunteered by many responding to the survey.
- The bibliographies of every gun book that had any reference to Remington were checked for additional sources. This collection of resource material was ferreted out while waiting for survey forms to come in.
- As the responses came in, chronological sorting of the dated entries began. (Without dates, duplicated entries would just help confuse the issues.) A spreadsheet was developed that allowed listing of "Serial number prefix, Serial number, Serial number suffix, Caliber, Barrel length, Markings on top of Barrel/frame, Number of Screws, Number of Pins, Finish, Engraved (yes or no), Split-Breech (yes or no), Grips (type of material used), Submission Date on Survey Form (or date of observation), and last, but not least, a remarks column.
- Spreadsheets were established for each caliber and one for the special configuration Long Barrel/Pocket/Buggy/Bicycle Rifles. The forms requested the responder's name, address, phone and fax numbers, as well as e-mail address. Actually, the submissions were recorded on a master composite spreadsheet, and the separate sheets were sorted from the master.
- Listing all entries sequentially by serial number on a composite form revealed some special circumstances and idiosyncrasies. It was the master spreadsheet that revealed the initial duplicate serial numbers that did not check out.
- Special characteristics just seemed to jump right off the printed page, e.g., brass frame, barrels that deviated from "normal" length, and a pistol with four pins when others its size had two screws and two pins.
- Pistol serial numbers with a prefix or suffix were immediately obvious.

- Topics to be used as possible chapter titles were developed, and separate files were established.
- Numerous notes, letters, postcards, e-mail messages and phone calls were launched. Similar communications that had been received had to be responded to, ensuring resolution of conflicting information.
- Available resource material was compared with anyone willing.
- The best research tool is hands-on inspection.
- Trial-and-error disassembly and reassembly sure exercised the brain as well as the fingers. This really helped to catalog all of the pieces (parts, that is!). It also facilitated surveying interchangeability of component parts.
- Don't be shy about asking for assistance or taking advantage of offers from others willing to give assistance.
- Attempt to rectify and/or clarify confusing issues and obvious discrepancies as they occur.
- Utilization of the Internet. Talk about a storehouse of knowledge, coupled with e-mail, it is awesome.
- Time had to be provided to document every conversation concerning Vest Pocket Pistols as soon as possible after they took place.
- Copies of all applicable patents had to be procured. Advertising samples, catalogs and source material were sought. My present personal firearms library of Remington resource material has grown from several copies of gun magazines, a couple years' supply of *Remington Society of America Journals* and a copy of Charlie Semmer's book to the bibliography herein.
- Material had to be developed to serve as backup for inclusion as Appendices.
- Talked to everyone who would listen and listened to everyone who would share their knowledge of Remington information, especially Vest Pocket Pistols and related subjects.
- Habit had to be developed to write down every thought even remotely relative to Vest Pocket Pistols, the minute it occurred.
- Time was devoted to the detailed inspection of magnified photographs, drawings and diagrams of Vest Pocket Pistols, as well as to examining every nook and cranny of the actual pistols, magnified as large as possible.
- Retention of disbelief of every facet of research until totally satisfied with verifiable proof, was difficult but necessary.
- Questionable information has to be approached from as many perspectives as possible.
- Illustrations and photographic images reflecting actual size keeps things in proper perspective.
- Identifiy the source and acquisition date of every newly acquired bit of information when it is received.
- Relentlessly pursue as much detailed information as time and resources allow.
- Accepting a steady diet of Remington Vest Pocket Pistols for a few years was not difficult. The motto was: "Eat, Drink and Sleep Remington Vest Pocket Pistols."
- Quite late in this endeavor a computer software program was discovered that allows the researcher to use the Internet to delve into libraries around the world to seek resource material on whatever subject desired. Limited experience in this area restricts detailed information. As soon as more expertise is acquired, an attempt will be made to share what promises to be a real boon to research of all types.
- Take nothing for granted.

QUESTION EVERYTHING!!

Copies of the three Research Survey forms utilized during this project are reproduced on the next five pages.

Remington Vest Pocket Pistol

RESEARCH SURVEY FORM

Remington Vest Pocket Pistol **Serial #** ____________________

Caliber: **.22RF:** ___ **.30RF:** ___ **.32RF:** ___

.41RF: ___ **Buggy Rifle:** ___ **Other:** ___ **(Please specify:** ____________**)**

Barrel Length: ______________________

Markings on Top of barrel & frame: ______________________________________

____

Number of Screws and Pins in Frame: **Screws:** ___ **Pins:** ___

Finish: **Blue:** ___ **Silver Plated:** ___ **Nickel:** ___ **Gilt:** ___

Other: ___ **(Please specify:** ____________**)**

Engraved: **Yes:** ___ **No:** ___

Split Breech: **Yes:** ___ **No:** ___

Grips: **Walnut:** ___ **Ivory:** ___ **Pearl:** ___

Other: ___ **(Please specify:** ____________ **)**

Please fill out completely, (use reverse side of page for any additional pertinent information or comments about your Vest Pocket Remington or suggestions on how to improve this form, etc.)

Submitted by: ______________________________ **Date:** ______________

Address: ____

City/State/Zipcode: ____

Please Mail Completed Form to : **Bob Hatfield, P.O. Box 586, Lake Ozark, MO 65049-0586**

Remington Vest Pocket Pistol

RESEARCH SURVEY FORM

(Revised 03/97)

Remington Vest Pocket Pistol **Serial #** ____________

Caliber: **.22RF:** ___ **.30RF:** ___ **.32RF:** ___ **.41RF:** ___ **Buggy Rifle:** ___ **Other:** ___ **(Please Specify:** ___ **)**

Barrel Length: ____________

Markings on Top of barrel & frame: ____________

____

Location of Markings: **Near breech:** ___ **On barrel:** ___

Direction of markings: **Breech to muzzle:** ___ **Muzzle to breech:** ___

Number of Screws and Pins in Frame: **Screws:** ___ **Pins:** ___

Finish: **Blue:** ___ **Silver Plated:** ___ **Nickel:** ___ **Gilt:** ___ **Other:** ___ **(Please specify:** ___ **)**

Engraved: **Yes:** ___ **No:** ___

Split Breech: **Yes:** ___ **No:** ___

Grips: **Walnut:** ___ **Rosewood:** ___ **Ivory:** ___ **Pearl:** ___ **Other:** ___ **(Please specify:** ___ **)**

Comments ____________

____

____

____

____

Please fill out completely, (use reverse side of page for any additional pertinent information or comments about your Vest Pocket Remington or suggestions on how to improve this form, etc.) Feel Free to submit a photograph of your Vest Pocket Remington. (Indicate your approval for the photo(s) to be used as long as you are identified as the source (Sorry, photos can not be returned)

Submitted by: ____________ **Date:** ____________

Address: ____________

City/State/Zipcode: ____________

Phone#:(____) ____________ **FAX#:**(____) ____________

E-Mail Address: ____________

Please Mail Completed Form to : **Bob Hatfield, P.O. Box 586, Lake Ozark, MO 65049-0586**

Remington Vest Pocket Pistol Research Survey Form

To make sure all measurements are taken the same way please follow these guidelines

(Measure barrel as illustrated, from breech-end to muzzle

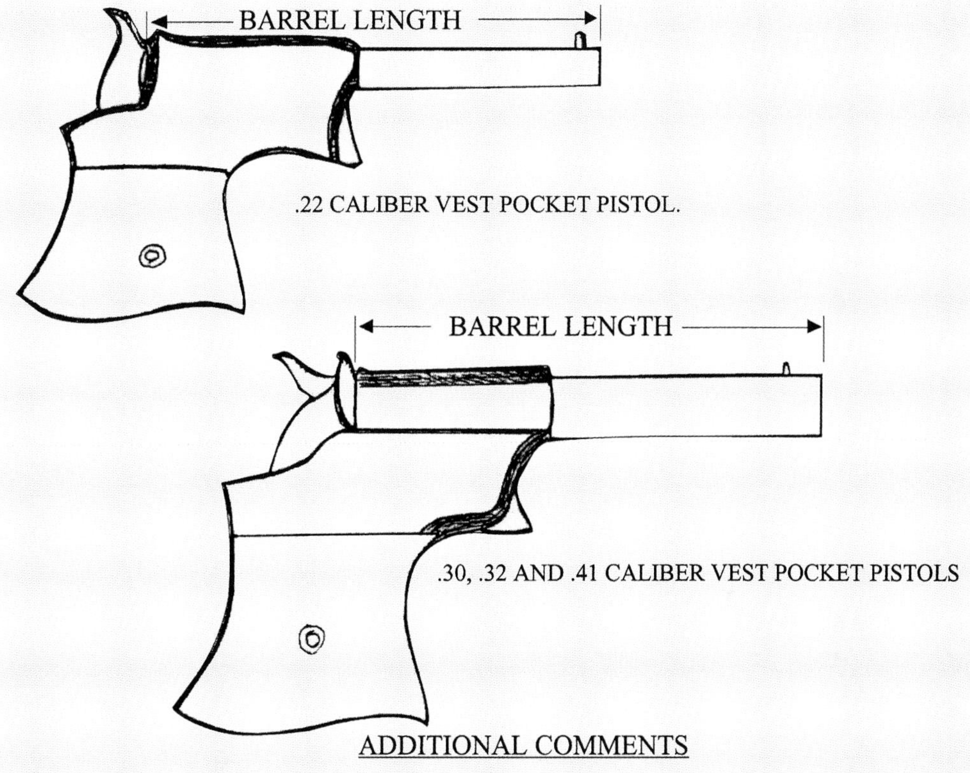

ADDITIONAL COMMENTS

HATFIELD, LTD
P.O. Box 586
Lake Ozark, MO 65049
Phone (573) 365-4234
Fax (573) 365-4235
Member Remington Society of America

Remington Vest Pocket Pistol
RESEARCH SURVEY FORM
(Revised 12/99)

Remington Vest Pocket Pistol **Serial #** ____________________

Caliber: **.22RF:** ___ **.30RF:** ___ **.32RF:** ___ **.41RF:** ___ **Buggy Rifle:** ___ **Other:**___(**Please Specify:**___)

Barrel Length: ________________________ *(SEE MEASURING GUIDE ON REVERSE SIDE)*

Markings on Top of barrel & frame: ____

____

Location of Markings: **Near breech:** ___ **On barrel:** ___

Direction of markings: **Breech to muzzle:** ___ **Muzzle to breech:** ___

Number of Screws and Pins in Frame: **Screws:** ___ **Pins:** ___ *(Do not count grip screw)*

Finish: **Blue:** ___ **Silver Plated:** ___ **Nickel:** ___ **Gilt:** ___ **Other:** ___ **(Please specify:** ________**)**

Engraved: **Yes:** ___ **No:** ___

Split Breech: **Yes:** ___ **No:** ___

Grips: **Walnut:** ___ **Rosewood:** ___ **Ivory:** ___ **Pearl:** ___ **Other:** ___

Comments ____

____

____

____

____

Please fill out completely, *(use reverse side of page for any additional pertinent information or comments about your Vest Pocket Remington or suggestions on how to improve this form, etc.) Feel Free to submit a photograph of your Vest Pocket Remington. (Indicate your approval for the photo(s) to be used as long as you are identified as the source (Sorry, photos can not be returned)*

Submitted by: ______________________________ **Date:** ______________

Address: ____

City/State/Zipcode: ____

Phone#:(____**)** ____________________ **FAX#:(**____**)** ______________

E-Mail Address: ______________________________

Please Mail Completed Form to : **Bob Hatfield, P.O. Box 586, Lake Ozark, MO 65049-0586**
Phone (573) 365-4234 Fax(573) 365-4235 E-mail bobhat@lakeozarks.net

Remington Vest Pocket Pistol Research Survey Form

To make sure all measurements are taken the same way please follow these guidelines

(Measure barrel as illustrated, from breech-end to muzzle

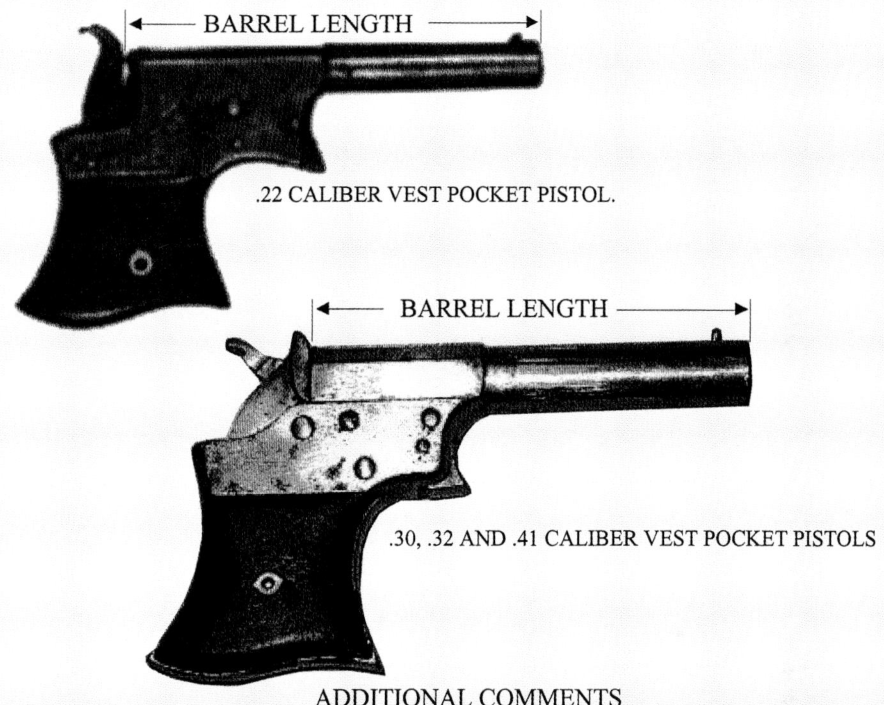

ADDITIONAL COMMENTS

Your Help is Needed!

REMINGTON FIREARMS RESEARCH

What do you know?

If you own an antique, collectible Remington firearm, you probably already know that detailed historical information may be difficult to find. Questions such as these aren't so simple to answer:

When was my Remington pistol or rifle made?

How many of them were manufactured? or

Did they all have 6-inch barrels?

Paper trails for some other American firearms manufacturers have survived. Production records have been retained and are relatively easy to locate. Considerable amounts of Colt and Winchester information are readily available. Some of their existing records divulge identification of variations as well as historical shipping records. In others, you can find specific series of serial numbers, and dates of manufacture of various models and/or variations. Not so with many of the antique/collectible Remington firearms.

For military firearms, factory records may be verified with governmental firearm orders, shipping documents and dated lists reflecting distribution to individual units. This is really helpful, and when there are factory records to start with, research is so much easier.

Availability of manufacturing dates, serial number sequences and quantities helps provide a solid foundation for research. Remington factory production records of many of their 19th-century firearms no longer exist.

Seeking historical data on the Remington Vest Pocket Pistols, for example, is like looking for the proverbial needle in the haystack. Researching these small weapons is hampered by the lack of historical production and distribution information.

The research/survey phase of the Remington Vest Pocket Pistol effort would have been more difficult, if not impossible, without the support and assistance received from others. Distribution of the Vest Pocket Research Survey Forms by Roy Marcot (they were mailed with the *RSA Journal*) provided much-needed exposure to Remington enthusiasts and collectors.

As soon as the request for information had been disseminated, collectors responded rapidly. Communicating with other Remington collectors has been quite beneficial. As a group, we Remington collectors need to continue to encourage expansion of both interest and membership in the Remington Society of America as well as expanded research studies on more models and varieties of Remington firearms.

As interest increases, communication will be improved. That interest and knowledge will also generate increased value for our collectibles. When additional Remington collectors are identified, our database will become more extensive. Shared information will also help to increase interest in antique and collectible Remington products.

What can you do?

Become active in the Remington Society of America. Take a more active role in Remington Research. Share what you know while finding out more about your treasures.

If you are not on the Internet, do yourself a favor and get signed on. There are many gun collector web sites to visit. When you make your interests known, you will find many people eager to share their knowledge, and they are anxious to learn from you, as well. Much research has been completed and some of it has resulted in on-going projects. Efforts are being made to document as much detail as possible about Remington antique and collectible firearms and associated products. All of this research requires more involvement, by all of us.

There are a number of antique and collectible Remington firearms enthusiasts who are really trying to lend a helping hand. They readily share their knowledge as they research their particular favorites. Those doing Remington Firearms research, that I am aware of, are listed below:

- Fritz Baehr, Charter President of the Remington Society of America, is working on Remington New Model Pocket Revolvers and Conversions. Fritz will send an appropriate Remington New Model Pocket Questionnaire to those who wish to have one. Whatever you have to share on this subject, contact: Fritz Baehr, 3125 Fremont Avenue, Boulder, CO 80304. Phone (303) 443-2691 or (303) 938-9093; Fax (303) 938-9094; e-mail: mooseb@worldnet.att.net
- Jay Huber, RSA Director, (The person responsible for organizing those great RSA Meetings and Seminars) has several research interests: Remington catalogs and advertising, as well as Remington Double Barrel Shotguns, Remington Knives, Civil War Handguns and Conversions. Share your knowledge on those subjects with Jay. Here's his address: Jay Huber, 1430 W. 57th Court, Ft. Lauderdale, FL. Phone: (954) 772-7133; Fax (954) 489-9538; e-mail: jayrem@aol.com
- Ken Domina is concentrating on Whitney Percussion Revolvers and Whitney Navy Conversions. Ask him for a copy of his research survey form. His address is: Ken Domina, 1402 Weber Ave., Ritzville, WA 99169.
- Dr. Harry Parker's focus is on the three Remington Smoot Patents and the Number 4 Revolvers. Contact him at: Dr. Harry J. Parker, 12023 Fieldwood Lane, Dallas, TX 75244. Phone (972) 233-8823; Fax (972) 385-7054.
- E.J. Williams and James Barnard are conducting ongoing research on the "Remington Double Derringer," a.k.a. Over/Under or Model 95, and the UMCC/UMC/Remington .41 rimfire Cartridge. Get your data concerning your Remington o/u Derringers to: E.J. Williams, 812 Roche de Bouef Court, Waterville, OH 43566; Phone (419) 878-3118. And/or James Barnard, 2359 E. Crestmont Lane, Littleton, CO 80126; Phone (303) 791-6068.
- Charlie Semmer, whose book on Remington Double Barrel Shotguns has already been published, will never be satisfied with what he has already found out about the side-by-sides. Share information on your Remington Double Barrel Shotgun(s) with Charlie. You may reach him at: Charles Semmer, 7885 Cyd Drive, Denver, CO 80221-3834; Phone: (303) 429-6947; e-mail: csemmer@mindspring.com
- John Gyde (Treasurer, Remington Society of America) is working on a book on Remington .22s. Let John in on what you know about them. Here's his address: John Gyde, 83362 Enterprise, Creswell, OR 97426; Phone: (541) 895-2862; e-mail: gydemate@aol.com
- Roger Philips is researching .46, .45, and .44 Remington revolver conversions for publication purposes. Get in touch with Roger at: Roger Philips, 22 Kensington Crescent, Regina, Saskatchewan, Canada S4S 7G5; Phone (306) 789-0706; e-mail: rbrooke@unibase.unibase.com
- Leon Wier, Jr., his eminence, Ol' RemShots himself, no less, our RSA President is recording serial numbers of Remington Models 1875s, 1888s and 1890s. Send your serial numbers for those models to: Leon Wier, Jr., 8268 Lone Feather Lane, Las Vegas, NV 89123; Phone (702) 896-9283; e-mail: lwierjr@aol.com
- Bob Creamer is collecting data on engraved Remington Model 8 and Model 81 Autoloading Rifles. He specifically wants Model, Caliber, Serial Number, level of engraving and if the engraving is signed. Send your engraved Model 8 and Model 81 information to: Bob Creamer,

1440 Wallace Road NW, Salem, OR 97304. Phone (503) 588-2080; e-mail: creamer10@home.com

- Mike Strietbeck is doing a survey on Remington Revolving Rifles. His research form was included in with the 4th Quarter *RSA Journal*. Whatever information you have on Remington Revolving Rifles, send it to: Mike Strietbeck, 26425 Sandy Creek, Lake Forest, CA 92630. Fax (714) 850-1013; e-mail: mstrietbeck@mammothproducts.com
- Don Ware is accumulating information on the Remington .44 caliber Army and .36 caliber Navy Civil War era models. If you have any data on these fascinating percussion pistols, please share it with Don. Write to him or send him an E-mail: Don Ware, 115 Foothill Lane, Russellville, AR 72801. e-mail: donlware@juno.com
- George Slatten is working on research on the Remington Model 12 slide action .22 rifles. Please share what you know about the Model 12s with George. Contact him at: George Slatten, P.O. Box 466, Derry, NH 03038. Phone: (603) 432-6880; e-mail: gls@mediaone.net
- Eugene Myszkowski, author of *The Remington-Lee Rifle* continues his research on the modern Remington Auto and Pump Rifles, Model 740 and Model 760. Contact Gene at: Gene Myszkowski, 33 Lindenwald Ave., Stuyvesant Fall, NY 12174-0167. Phone: (518) 799-5171; e-mail: genejan61@berk.com
- Roy Marcot (Our *RSA Journal* editor) has undertaken a research project on Remington Rolling Block Rifles. He will appreciate whatever information and material you can provide concerning these intriguing rifles. Roy may be contacted at: Roy Marcot, 12458 E. Ft. Lowell Road, Tucson, AZ 85749. Phone: (520) 760-0716; e-mail: roymarcot@msn.com
- John F. Lacy is doing research on Remington Models: 7, 30, 600, 660, 700, XP 100, 788 and Mohawk. Share your information on these Remington models with John. Here's how to contact him: John F. Lacy, 809 W. Stone, Brenham, TX 77833. Phone (409) 836-1552; e-mail: slacy@phoenix.net
- Robert W. Pryor is accumulating data on the Remington Model 51. This semi-auto pistol was made in .32 cal. and .380 cal. Contact Bob and give all the support you can: Robert W. Pryor, 1344 Blackfield Drive, Santa Clara, CA 95051-3911. Phone: (408) 296-0404; e-mail: rwpryor3@home.com

…and of course, whatever data you may have concerning Remington Vest Pocket Pistols (serial numbers, photographs, advertising, etc.) send to: Bob Hatfield, P.O. Box 586, Lake Ozark, MO 65049. Phone: (573)-365-4234; Fax (573)-365-4235; e-mail: bobhat@usmo.com

Special Memorial

J. Wayne Matthews, a valued RSA Member, passed away in July 2000. He was actively conducting extensive research on the Double Barrel Remington Derringers. He was always happy to share his findings and his knowledge with everyone. He will be missed by us all.

Do it, Now!

If you own any of the aforementioned Remington antique and collectible firearms, get involved. Take a more active part. You can help resolve some of the unanswered questions about their past. Contact your friends who are doing the research. Provide them with as much historical data as you can. Join in the effort to perpetuate interest in antique Remington firearms.

We'll all be glad you did!

Appendices

Appendix 1

Estimated Dates of Manufacture

Conclusion found in Chapter 5...1863 through 1888.

Dates of Manufacture	Source
1865–1888	Ball, 95
1863–1867	Bowman, '53
c.1865–1888	Flayderman, '94
1865–1888	Hatch, '56
c.1865–1888	Kirkland, '88
1866–1886	Madaus, '97
1865–1888	Peterson, '66
Production started sometime during the Civil War	Marcot, '98
1865–1888	Schwing, '96
1865–1888 *(.22 cal.)*	Wier, '94
1865 to at least 1876 *(Larger calibers)*	Wier, '96

Appendix 2

Quantities Produced

Conclusion found in Chapter 3.

Quantity Estimate	Caliber	Source
10,000	.30, .32 and .41	Ball, '95
25,000	.22	Flayderman, '94
10,000 or less	.30, .32 and .41	
25,000 plus	All	Hatch, '56
25,000	.22	Kirkland '88
About 10,000	.30, .32 and .41	
16,500	.22	Madaus, '97
16,500	.30, .32 and .41	
20,000	.30, .32 and .41	Marcot, '98
50,000	All	Peterson, '66
15,000	.22	Shaffer, '97
2,800	.30	
3,000 to 3,500	.32	
About 5,000	.41	
About 25,000	.22	Schwing, '96
10,000	.30, .32 and .41	
25,000	.22	Wier, '94
10,000	.30, .32 and .41	Wier, '96

Appendix 3

Serial Numbers Reported

Information concerning the "Buggy Rifle" versions of the Remington Vest Pocket Pistols has been collected and is being reported separately due to their unique configurations. Some involve components of two different pistol, e.g., .22 caliber barrels attached to medium or large caliber frames.

Serial numbers collected during this research effort are from several sources. Many have been personally observed by the author. Others were submitted by owners/collectors or as lists of observations over many years by avid, curious collectors.

Total Number of Serial Numbers in This Study **362**

BREAKDOWN BY CALIBER:

Caliber	SN Range	No. of specimens	Percentage*
.22 Caliber Rimfire Short	1–84,575	174	48%
.30 Caliber Rimfire Short	2–10,790	42	12%
.32 Caliber Rimfire Short	40–3513	30	8%
.41 Caliber Rimfire Short	13–10866	103	28%
Long Barrel and/or Wire Stock Buggy Rifles	129–4773	13	4%
TOTALS		**362**	**100%**

**Rounded off to the nearest full percentage.*

Appendix 3A

Percentage of Serial Numbers Reported by Caliber

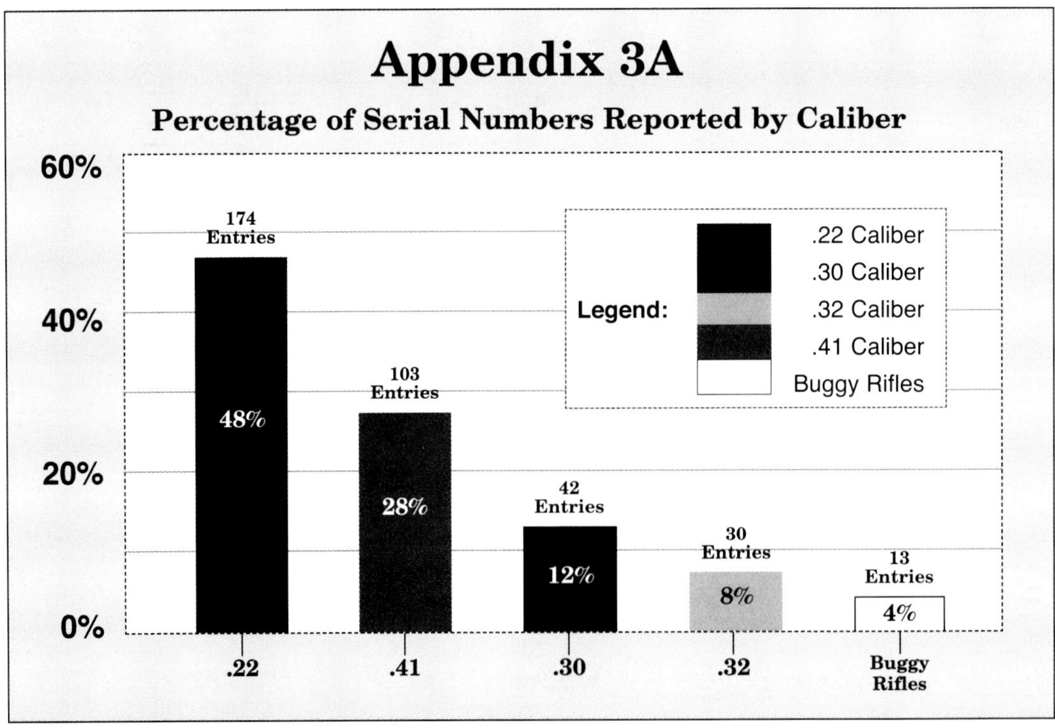

Appendix 4

Remington Vest Pocket Pistol Specifications

	No. 1 Size	No. 2 Size		No. 3 Size
Caliber:	.22 Rimfire Short	.30 Rimfire Short	.32 Rimfire Short	.41 Rimfire Short
Frame Size:	No. 1 Size	No. 2 Size	No. 2 Size	No. 3 Size
Number of Shots:	1	1	1	1
Overall length:	4.25 inches	4.5625 inches	5.125 inches	5.25 inches
Barrel length:	3.25, 3.75 & 4 inches	3, 3.25, 3.5, 3.75 3.875 & 4 inches	4.375 inches	4 & 4.125 inches
Rifling:	5 grooves	5 grooves	5 grooves	5 grooves
Markings:	REMINGTON'S ILION. N.Y. PATENT OCT.1, 1861	REMINGTON'S ILION. N.Y. PATD OCT.1,1861, NOV.15,1864	REMINGTON'S ILION. N.Y. PATD OCT.1,1861,NOV.15,1864	REMINGTON'S ILION. N.Y. PATD OCT.1,1861,NOV.15,1864
Markings Location:	Top of Barrel	Top of Barrel	Top of Barrel	Top of Barrel
Serial Number Location:	Underside of Bbl. & under left grip	Underside of Bbl. & under left grip	Underside of Bbl. & under left grip	Underside of Bbl. & under left grip
Number of Screws:	2	4	4	2
Number of Pins:	2	1	1	3
Trigger:	Sheath	Sheath	Sheath	Sheath
Sights: Front Rear	Brass Pin Groove in frame	Brass Pin Groove in frame	Brass Pin Groove in frame	Brass Pin Groove in frame
Grips:	Walnut Rosewood Pearl Ivory	Walnut Rosewood Pearl Ivory	Walnut Rosewood Pearl Ivory	Walnut Rosewood Pearl Ivory
Finish:	Blue Nickel Plate Silver Plate Gold Gilt	Blue Nickel Plate Silver Plate	Blue Nickel Plate Silver Plate	Blue Nickel Plate Silver Plate
Engraved:	Special Order	Special Order	Special Order	Special Order
Split Breech:	No	Yes	Yes	Yes
Weight:	3.875 ounces	6.75 ounces	7.375 ounces	11 ounces

Appendix 5

Remington Vest Pocket Pistols
No. 1 Size — .22 Rimfire Short

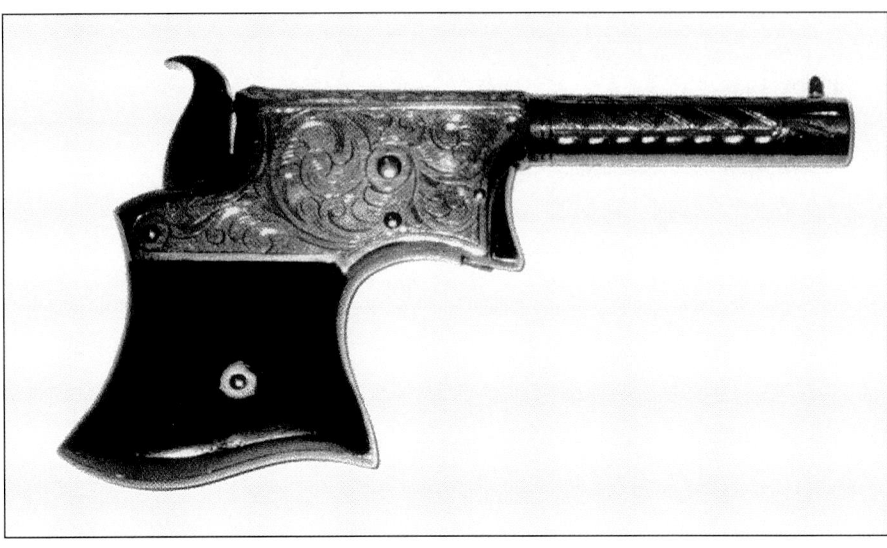

.22 Caliber Remington Vest Pocket Pistol, SN15129, silver finish, rosewood grips, engraved. (Elliott L. Burka Photo)

The first of the Remington Vest Pocket Pistols was the diminutive .22 Caliber Rimfire Short Model, built on a No. 1 Size Frame. This unique flat pistol has only 16 parts. They are listed in Appendix **5A "PARTS LIST,"** which also illustrates the general appearance of each part. The exploded view is accompanied by identification of the individual parts.

Appendix **5B "DO-IT-YOURSELF PRECAUTIONS"** contains sage advice to the collector. Unintentional abuse can be costly. So, as the story goes, "A word to the wise..."

Appendix **5C "DISASSEMBLY AND REASSEMBLY"** provides easy-to-follow guidelines for those who must answer the urge to take stuff apart and attempt to put it back together again.

Photographic identification of the disassembled parts is provided in Appendix **5D "COMPONENT PARTS."**

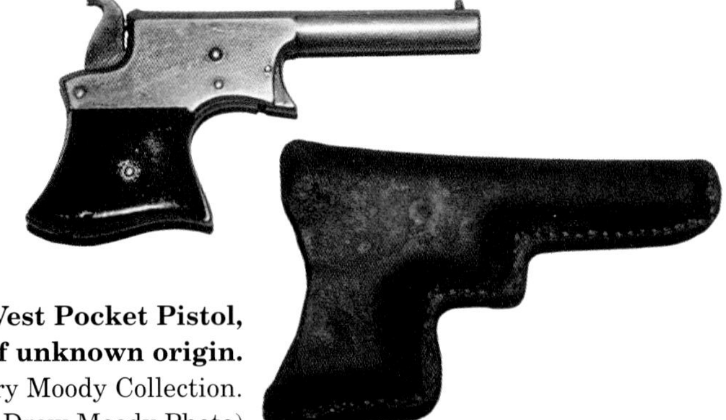

.22 Caliber Remington Vest Pocket Pistol, SN2298, shown with holster of unknown origin. (R.S.A. Member Larry Moody Collection. Drew Moody Photo)

Appendix 5A

Remington Vest Pocket Pistol
No. 1 Size — .22 Caliber Rimfire Short

PARTS LIST

1. Barrel/Receiver
2. Trigger
3. Trigger Spring
4. Trigger Pin
5. Hammer Pin
6. Center Frame Screw
7. Rear Frame Screw
8. Grip Frame
9. Left Grip
10. Grip Screw
11. Left Grip Escutcheon
12. Main Spring
13. Right Grip Escutcheon
14. Right Grip
15. Hammer
16. Front Sight Post

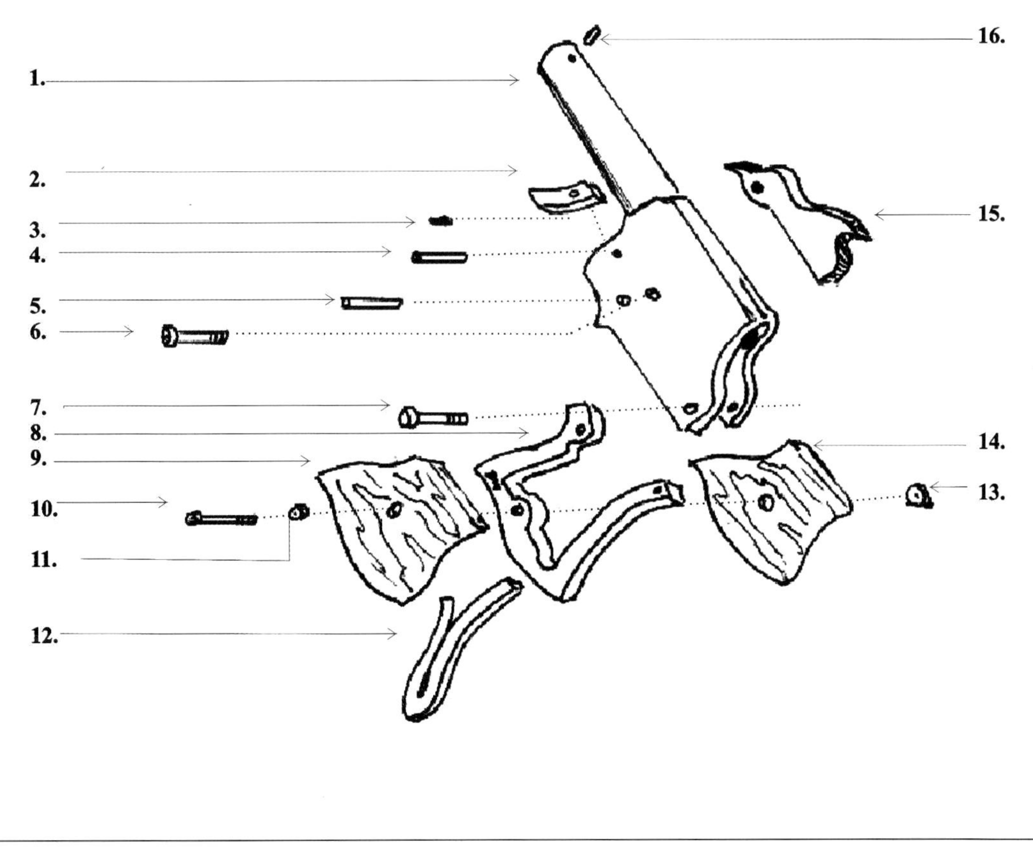

Appendix 5B

Do-It-Yourself Precautions

These precautions apply, in general, to all sizes and calibers of Remington Vest Pocket Pistols and, for that matter, to any and all antique firearms.

Before you initiate a fact-finding dismantling operation to delve into the mechanical mysteries of your Remington Vest Pocket Pistol, consider the following:

The valuable collectible you have there may just resist investigative violation. As good as Remington screws were made, they surrender their crisp shoulders when excessive force is applied. In many instances, years of exposure to the air and moisture created rust on the thread developing an unseen lock, resulting from remaining in a constant position, as the oxidation built up.

Even though you may get the urge to learn all about these small wonders by disassembly, then attempting reassembly, think first. Assure yourself that it won't matter if you can't get it back together properly. Unless you feel you are qualified to take 'em apart and put 'em back together again, resist the urge. Take my word for it, just encountering all of the pieces (parts) testify to the genius of their designers. Respect for the inventors develops immediately.

For the untrained novice with little or no idea of which screw or pin to remove first, each step of disassembly will present a challenge. Unless you possess the skills of a trained and practiced gunsmith, detail stripping is not recommended. You could diminish the value of your treasure.

Exploded views of each size Remington Vest Pocket Pistol are contained in this volume. The nomenclature of the parts has been discussed with others and compared with an old Remington catalog listing. Also included are disassembly and reassembly guidance in simple easy-to-read form. Both of these elements are the result of numerous (reasonably successful) dismantling escapades. They are not to be misinterpreted as encouragement for you to go on a dismantling spree.

However, if you are compelled to experience the adventure of taking stuff apart and attempting to get them back together again, first arm yourself with the proper tools and temperament. Screwdrivers that do not fit the slot in the head of a screw exactly can disfigure their appearance and utility. Scars resulting from excessive force will mar the appearance and diminish your pistol's value.

Improper selection of which punch to use to urge a retaining pin from its position can generate unwanted dents, scratches and dings. Undue pressure applied when trying to remove a spring can result in a broken spring. Let me tell you that replacement springs for Remington Vest Pocket Pistols are not readily available.

Close inspection of many of the collectible pistols that you will encounter will reveal evidence of amateur adventures or previous attempts to take them apart and put them back together again. After numerous times screwing and unscrewing, manipulations have a tendency to loosen the fit of the threads, or worse, strip the threads completely.

Retaining pins, pounded in and out (probably including a few tries in the wrong direction), tend to bend, chip and generally get disfigured. This really mars the appearance of a formerly polished domed surface. Such disfigurement will make your pistol look anything but pristine.

Our tiny examples of the gun makers' art have survived more than a century, and every little bit of abuse, regardless of how unintentional, leaves indelible scars. So please: HANDLE WITH CARE!!!

Appendix 5C

Disassembly/Reassembly of the Remington Vest Pocket Pistol No. 1 Size, .22 Caliber (Rimfire Short)

It is with a great deal of reluctance that this guide to disassembly and reassembly is even included. Though your curiosity may be satisfied, unless you possess natural gunsmithing skills, you could do irreparable damage to your valuable antique collectible firearm. However, if you feel that you really must "give it a go," the following should be of some assistance to you.

Materials and tools you will require:

- Set of Gun Screwdrivers
- Small Jar, Box, Pan or Tray
- Pliers (with unscored/smooth jaws)
- Set of Brass Punches
- Gun Oil
- Soft Cloth
- Table Cover (To protect both your Vest Pocket Pistol and your work surface)

In general, these instructions may also be applied to the larger-size "split-breech" model Vest Pocket Pistols, too!

With the aforementioned material and tools handy, you are ready to embark upon the task of taking your Vest Pocket Pistol apart.

To Disassemble:

FIRST... Check bore to assure that the pistol is unloaded.

THEN... Have your small box, jar, pan or tray handy...to put the parts in, as they are removed.

NEXT... Carefully select a screwdriver with a blade to fit the grip screw. Remove the grip screw and remove the grips (place the grip screw back into the grips to make certain that it does not get misplaced)...and then...Place the grips, connected with the grip screw into your handy parts container.

NOW... With a pair of pliers, compress the main spring and move the curved portion out of the frame and lift the spring out of the pistol. Place the mainspring in the parts container you have selected.

AGAIN... Select a screwdriver that fits the slot in the frame screws, then remove the frame screws.

FINALLY... Select a punch of appropriate size and gently remove the frame pins and the trigger pin. (Please note: if the screw heads are found on the left side of the frame, that should indicate that the pin may be removed by driving it gently from the right side out through the left side.)

NOW... While you have your treasure dismantled, clean it thoroughly. (Don't misunderstand, this DOES NOT mean that you should scour it with steel wool and/or abrasives!!!)

To Reassemble:

FIRST... Prior to reassembling your Vest Pocket Pistol, apply a light coat of gun oil to all of the pistol's parts.

THEN... Simply reverse the above procedure and put the pieces back where you found them.

Appendix 5D

Remington Vest Pocket Pistol
No. 1 Size, .22 Caliber (Rimfire Short)

COMPONENT PARTS

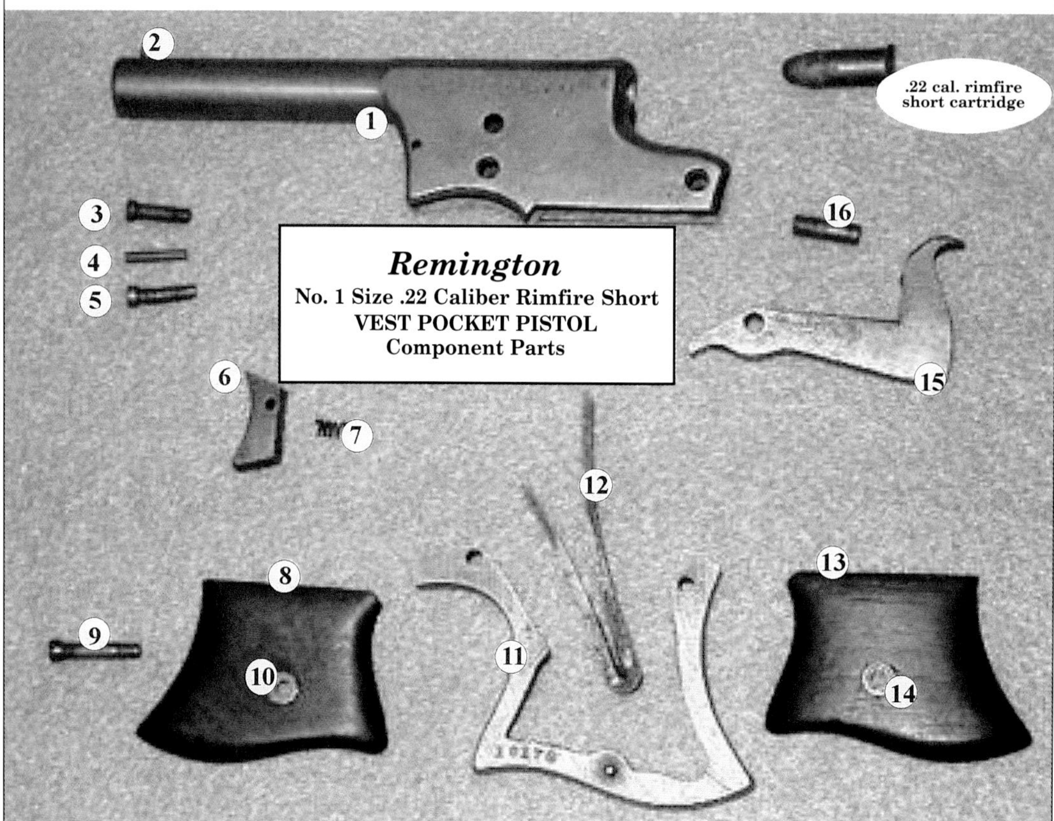

1. Barrel/Receiver
2. Front Sight Post
3. Top Frame Screw
4. Trigger Pin
5. Center Frame Screw
6. Trigger
7. Trigger Spring
8. Right Grip
9. Grip Screw
10. Right Grip Escutcheon
11. Grip Frame
12. Main Spring
13. Left Grip
14. Left Grip Escutcheon
15. Hammer
16. Hammer Pin

Appendix 6

Remington Vest Pocket Pistol
No. 2 Size, .30 and .32 Caliber (Rimfire Short)

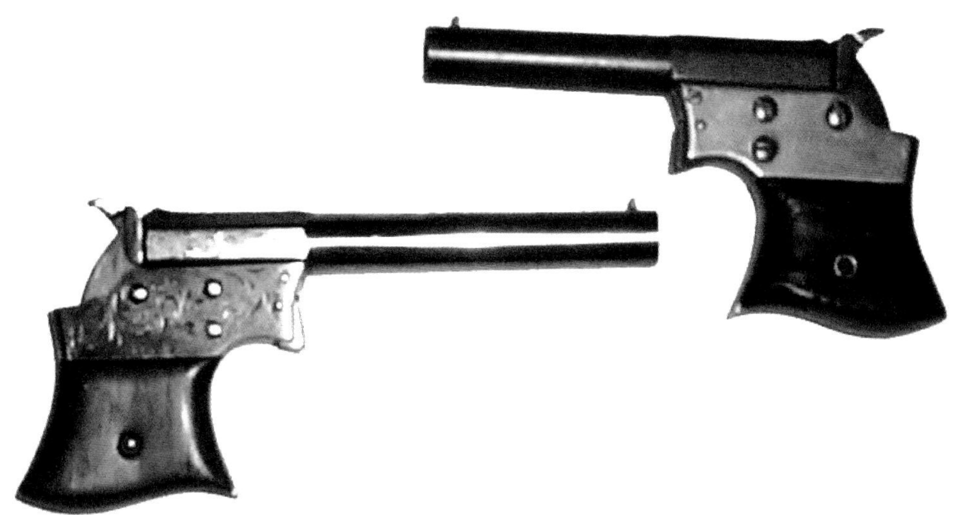

.30 Caliber Remington Vest Pocket Pistol, SN1540 *(Right)* **and .32 Caliber Remington Vest Pocket Pistol, SN191** *(Left).* (Author's Collection)

Different size frames were used to manufacture Remington Vest Pocket Pistols. But, the No. 2 Size was the only frame to be used to make more than one caliber model. Both .30 Caliber Rimfire Short and .32 Caliber Rimfire Short were made using the No. 2 Size Frame. These mid-size Vest Pocket Pistols contain 19 parts. They are interchangeable except for the barrels.

See Appendix **6A "PARTS LIST,"** which also illustrates the general appearance of each part. An exploded view is accompanied by identification of the individual parts.

- All of the cautions listed in Appendix **5B "DO-IT-YOURSELF PRECAUTIONS"** contain some sage advice to collectors, and also apply to the No. 2 Size Vest Pocket Pistols.
- Appendix **5C "DISASSEMBLY and REASSEMBLY…"** guidelines apply generally to the mid-size models, too!

Appendix 6A

Remington Vest Pocket Pistol
No. 2 Size, .30 and .32 Caliber (Rimfire Short)

PARTS LIST

1. Front Sight Post
2. .32 Caliber Barrel/Receiver
3. .30 Caliber Barrel/Receiver
4. Split Breech
5. Hammer
6. Rear Frame Screw
7. & 8. Right Grip & Escutcheon
9. Main Spring
10. Frame
11. & 12. Left Grip Escutcheon
13. Grip Screw
14. Trigger Spring
15. Lower Frame Screw
16. Trigger Pin
17. Trigger
18. Front Frame Screw
19. Upper Center Frame Screw

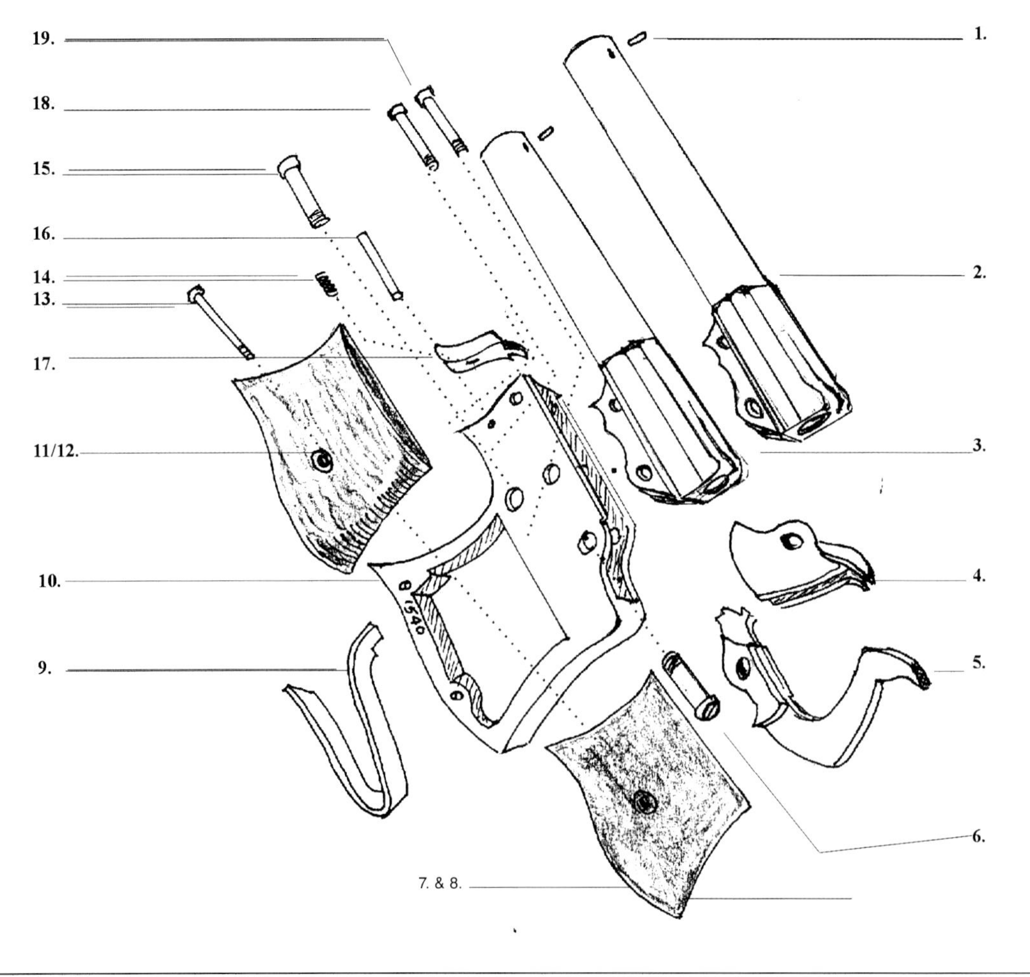

Appendix 6B

Remington Vest Pocket Pistol
No. 2 Size, .30 and .32 Caliber (Rimfire Short)

Special Note: Because of the interchangeability of parts in the .30 caliber and .32 caliber Vest Pocket Pistols, only the .32 is illustrated here! The barrels and the cartridges are different.

COMPONENTS PARTS

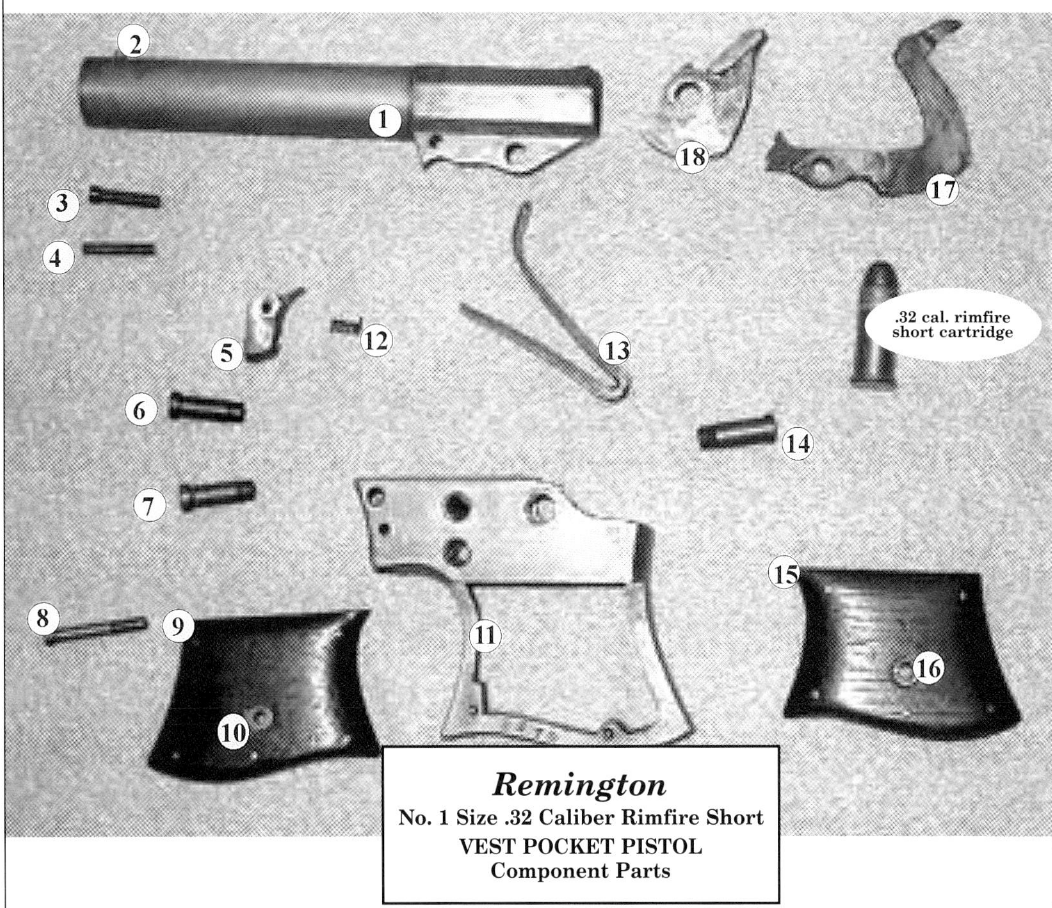

Remington
No. 1 Size .32 Caliber Rimfire Short
VEST POCKET PISTOL
Component Parts

1. Barrel/Receiver
2. Front Sight Post
3. Top Frame Screw
4. Trigger Pin
5. Trigger
6. Top Frame Screw
7. Lower Frame Screw
8. Grip Screw
9. Right Grip
10. Right Grip Escutcheon
11. Grip Frame
12. Trigger Spring
13. Main Spring
14. Rear Frame Screw
15. Left Grip
16. Left Grip Escutcheon
17. Hammer
18. Split Breech

Appendix 7

Remington Vest Pocket Pistol
No. 3 Size, .41 Caliber (Rimfire Short)

No. 3 Size frame was used by Remington to produce only .41 Caliber Rimfire Short Vest Pocket Pistols. These were the largest of the Vest Pocket Pistols containing 18 parts.

- See Appendix **7A "PARTS LIST,"** which also illustrates the general appearance of each part. An exploded view is accompanied by identification of the individual parts.

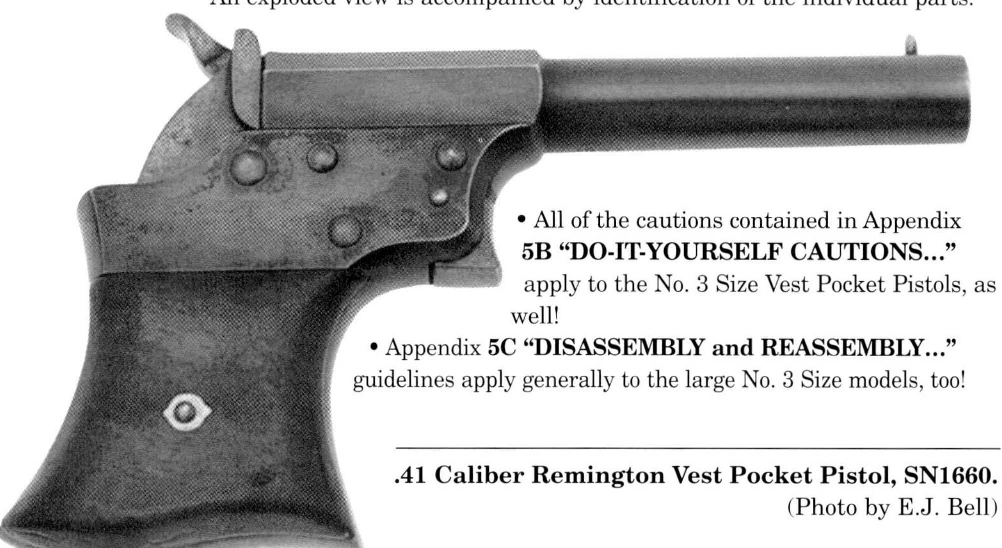

- All of the cautions contained in Appendix **5B "DO-IT-YOURSELF CAUTIONS..."** apply to the No. 3 Size Vest Pocket Pistols, as well!
- Appendix **5C "DISASSEMBLY and REASSEMBLY..."** guidelines apply generally to the large No. 3 Size models, too!

.41 Caliber Remington Vest Pocket Pistol, SN1660.
(Photo by E.J. Bell)

In the Remington Arms Museum in Ilion, New York, you will find two Remington .41 caliber rimfire short Vest Pocket Pistols. Serial number 1971 *(below)* **is a nickel-plated Vest Pocket with walnut grips and is marked with the common markings described in Chapter 6. The serial number was found under the left grip, near the toe, as well as on the underside of its 3.75-inch barrel.**

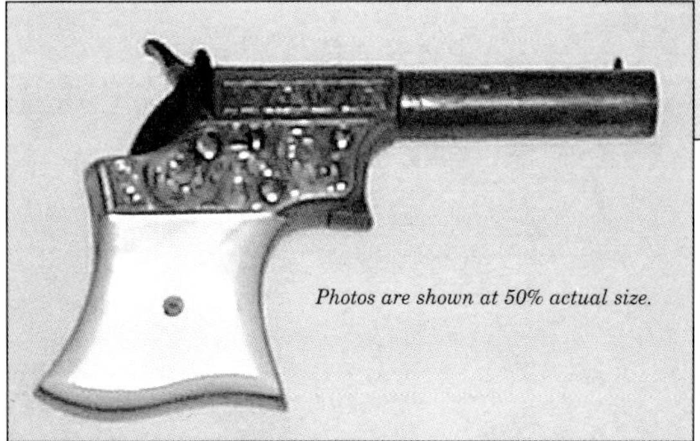

Photos are shown at 50% actual size.

The other .41 Vest Pocket Pistol, serial number 2415 *(left)*, **is nickel plated, factory engraved with picture-perfect pearl grips. The serial number on this one was found in the same locations as the aforementioned model. This one also has a 3.75-inch barrel.**

Appendix 7A

Remington Vest Pocket Pistol
No. 3 Size, .41 Caliber (Rimfire Short)

PARTS LIST

1. Front Sight Pin
2. .41 Cal. Barrel/Receiver
3. Trigger Spring
4. Trigger
5. Front Frame Screw
6. Trigger Pin
7. Lower Frame Pin
8. Frame
9. Grip Screw
10. Left Grip & Escutcheon
11. Wire Spring
12. Split Breech
13. Hammer
14. Rear Frame Pin
15. Center Frame Screw
16. Right Grip & Escutcheon
17. Bent Main Spring
18. Main Spring Extension

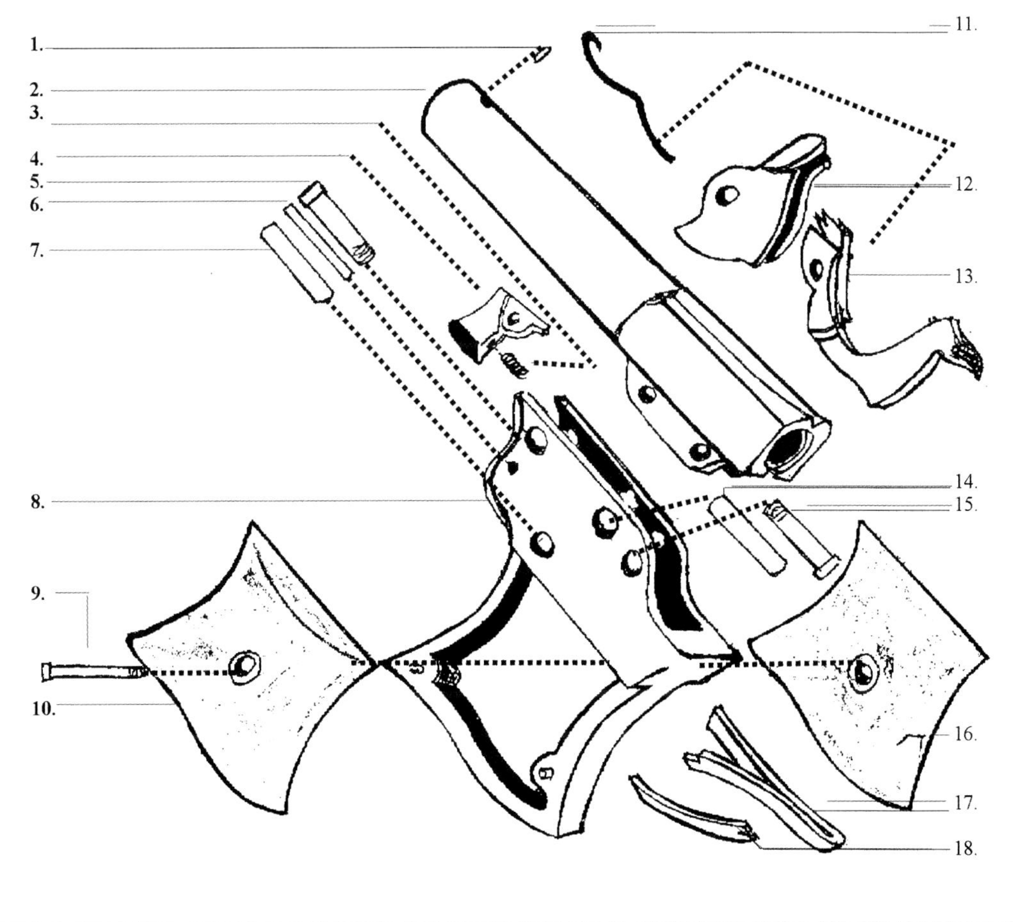

Appendix 7B

Remington Vest Pocket Pistol
No. 3 Size, .41 Caliber (Rimfire Short)

COMPONENT PARTS

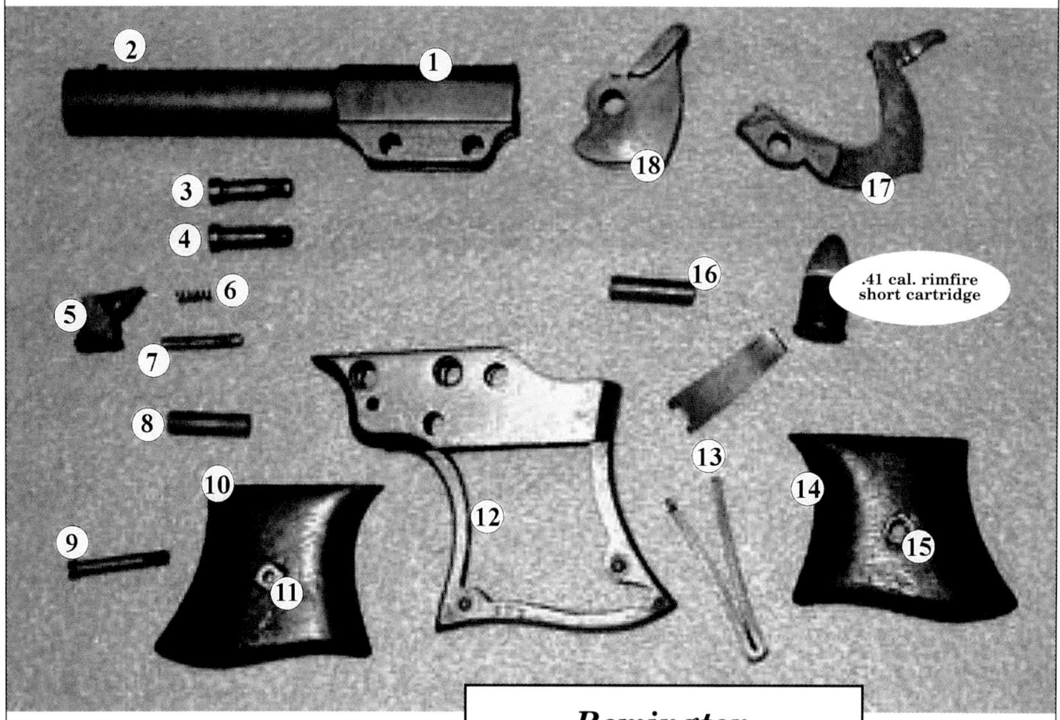

Remington
No. 3 Size .41 Caliber Rimfire Short
VEST POCKET PISTOL
Component Parts

1. **Barrel/Receiver**
2. **Front Sight Post**
3. **Top Frame Screw**
4. **Center Frame Screw**
5. **Trigger**
6. **Trigger Spring**
7. **Trigger Pin**
8. **Hammer Pin**
9. **Grip Screw**
10. **Right Grip**
11. **Right Grip Escutcheon**
12. **Frame**
13. **2-pc. Main Spring**
14. **Left Grip**
15. **Left Grip Escutcheon**
16. **Breech Pin**
17. **Hammer**
18. **Split Breech**

Appendix 8

PATENT INFORMATION

Copies of patents issued to William H. Elliot and Joseph Rider were ordered from the United States Patent Office in Washington, D.C. When a call went out for help, some were furnished by Ol' RemShots and other RSA Members. Those available have been reproduced and are included to illustrate the origins of the Remington Vest Pocket Pistols:

Patent Number	Issued to	Date
25,470	Joseph Rider	September 13, 1859
33,382	William H. Elliot	October 1, 1861
40,887	Joseph Rider	December 8, 1863
1,663*	Joseph Rider	* A reissue of May 3, 1864
45,123	Joseph Rider	November 15, 1864
53,543	Joseph Rider	March 27, 1866

Patent number 33,382, in actuality the Elliot design patent for "improvement in revolving firearms," included the basis for the fundamental design of the hammer used in the .22 cal. Remington Vest Pocket Pistol and is the patent identified by the information that appeared on the top of the barrel/receiver/frame of the .22 cal., No. 1 Size, Vest Pocket Pistols.

Patent number 45,123, the Joseph Rider patent, covers the introduction of the "Split-Breech Technology" built into the larger .30 and .32 caliber (No. 2 Size) Remington Vest Pocket Pistols and the .41 caliber (No. 3 Size) Remington models.

Both the Oct. 1, 1861, and the Nov. 15, 1864, patent information appears on the top of the receiver/barrel of the No. 2 and No. 3 Size Remington Split-Breech Vest Pocket Pistols.

Review the illustrations of the Barrel/Receivers for the No. 2 and the No. 3 Size Remington Vest Pocket Pistols in Chapter 6. Particularly noteworthy is the extension on the lower side of the receiver, as depicted and pointed out in the drawings reproduction of Patent Number 40,887.

The extension in that Patent drawing is not the same as the ones found on the Split-Breech models of the No. 2 or the No. 3 Size Vest Pockets encountered in this study.

Spring configurations in the Patent drawings are dissimilar to those found on surviving samples. The spur on the hammer was made larger when Remington manufactured their Vest Pocket Pistols. Front sight pins were added. They were absent in the Patent Drawings.

Appendix 8A

J. RIDER.

Breech-Loading Fire-Arm.

No. 25,470. Patented Sept. 13, 1859.

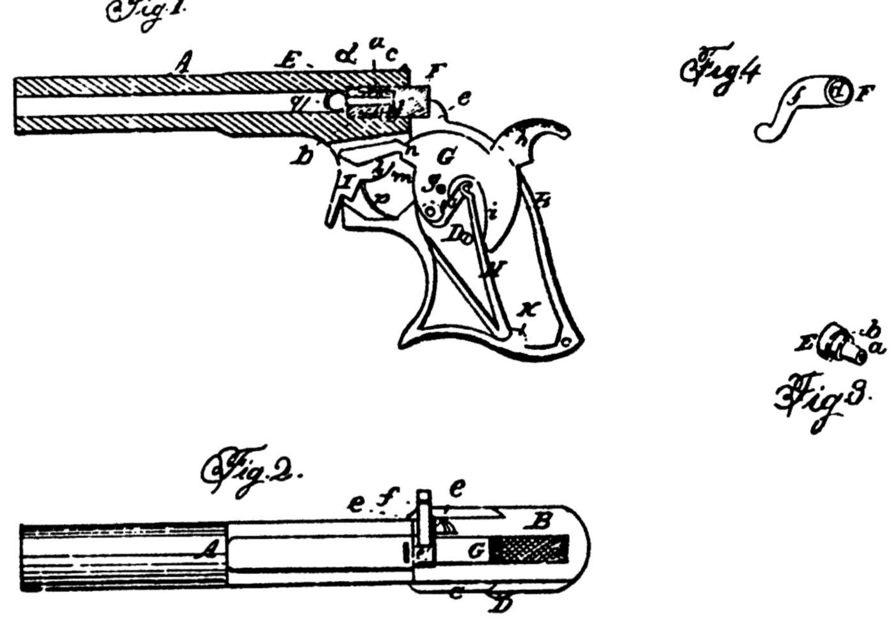

Witnesses:

Inventor:
Joseph Rider

UNITED STATES PATENT OFFICE.

JOSEPH RIDER, OF NEWARK, OHIO, ASSIGNOR TO HIMSELF AND E. REMINGTON & SONS, OF ILION, NEW YORK.

IMPROVEMENT IN BREECH-LOADING FIRE-ARMS.

Specification forming part of Letters Patent No. **25,470**, dated September 13, 1859.

To all whom it may concern:

Be it known that I, JOSEPH RIDER, of Newark, in the county of Licking and State of Ohio, have invented certain new and useful Improvements in Pistols; and I do hereby declare that the following is a full, clear, and exact description of the same, reference being had to the accompanying drawings, forming part of this specification, in which—

Figure 1 is a longitudinal central section of a pistol with my improvements. Fig. 2 is a top view of the same. Fig. 3 is a perspective view of what I call the "cap-tube." Fig. 4 is a front view of the breech-pin.

Similar letters of reference indicate corresponding parts in the several figures.

My invention consists in a novel combination of a movable breech-pin and tube for the reception of a percussion-cap applied to a pistol, as hereinafter described, for the purpose of employing for the charge the powder contained in the cap, and making a very convenient and efficient pistol of small size.

It further consists in a certain construction of the parts of the lock and arrangement thereof within the stock of the pistol, and in relation to the barrel, for the purpose of bringing the parts within a small compass.

To enable others skilled in the art to make and use my invention, I will proceed to describe its construction and operation.

A is the barrel, cast with or screwed into the stock B. On one side of the stock is a plate, C, made movable for the purpose of inserting the parts of and examining or oiling the lock, and secured in place by a screw, D. The barrel is open at the rear end, and counterbored to receive the cap-tube E and breech-pin F. The breech-pin F and the front portion of the cap-tube E are fitted snugly, but easily, into the counterbore of the barrel, so that they may be inserted and taken out without difficulty. The rear portion of the cap-tube is turned down much smaller than the front part to constitute the nipple *a*, for the reception of the percussion-cap *c*, Fig. 1, and in front of the nipple it is made rather larger than the exterior of the cap, as shown at *b* in Figs. 1 and 3, and this part *b* is fitted snugly but easily into a cavity, *d*, in the front of the breech-pin, said cavity being of a depth about equal to the length of the nipple and part *b* of the tube, so that the head of the cap, intervening between the end of the nipple and the back of the cavity, may prevent the whole of the part *b* entering the breech-pin. On one side of the breech-pin, close to its rear end, which projects from the counterbore of the barrel, there is a small lever, *f*, which is intended to drop into a notch, *e*, in one side of the stock, for the purpose of preventing the breech-pin and cap-tube dropping out from the counterbore of the barrel, and this notch *e* is wide enough to permit the breech-pin moving a short distance longitudinally.

G is the hammer, working upon the pin *g*, which occupies very nearly the same position as the hammer pin of other pistols. The hammer is of peculiar form, the lower part of the front of its thumb-piece *h* constituting the face, which strikes upon the rear end of the breech-pin and a cavity, *i i*, Fig. 1, being provided behind the pin *g* and between the said pin and the thumb-piece to receive the extremity of the V-shaped mainspring H, which is connected with the hammer below the pin *g* by a stirrup, *j*, and which is held in place between the front of the stock and a projection, *k*, Fig. 1, at the bottom thereof. I, Fig. 1, is the trigger, working upon the pin *l*, and carrying its own sear *m*, which engages with a notch, *n*, in the front part of the hammer. *p* is the trigger-spring.

To load, the hammer is cocked and the breech-pin F turned to free its lever *f* of the notch *e*, and then drawn out, bringing with it the cap-tube E. The cap-tube is then drawn out of the cavity of the breech-pin and the cap placed on the nipple, and the cap-tube is then replaced in the breech-pin, the ball *q* (represented in red color in Fig. 1) having been previously placed in the rear of the barrel. The firing may be then immediately effected by pulling the trigger, or the hammer may be let down gently upon the breech-pin till the piece is required to be fired, when it is to be recocked by drawing back the hammer. When the trigger is pulled, the hammer falls against the rear end of the breech-pin and drives the latter forward against the cap, and as the front end of the cap-tube bears against the front end of the counterbore of the barrel, the cap is exploded, and the force of the explosion being confined by the breech pin is all expended upon the ball, and causes it to be projected from the barrel.

The cap employed may be an ordinary per-

2 **25,470**

cussion-cap, or a cap with a stronger charge specially made for the purpose.

What I claim as my invention, and desire to secure by Letters Patent, is—

1. The combination of the movable breech-pin F and the cap-tube E, applied to a pistol, substantially as herein described.

2. In combination with a hammer of the form herein described, the arrangement of the mainspring and trigger relatively to each other, to the hammer, and to the stock and barrel, substantially as herein described.

JOSEPH RIDER.

Witnesses:

R. P. HARE,

JOHN HAEFLER.

Appendix 8B

PATENT DEPT. W. H. ELLIOT.

Revolver.

~~No. 2,378.~~
No. 33,382.

Patented Oct. 1, 1861.

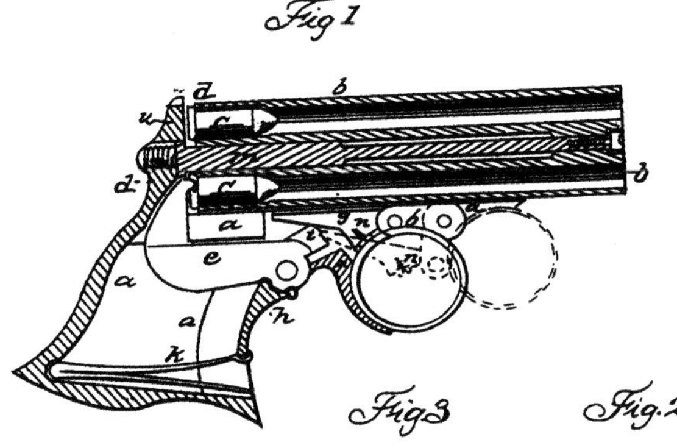

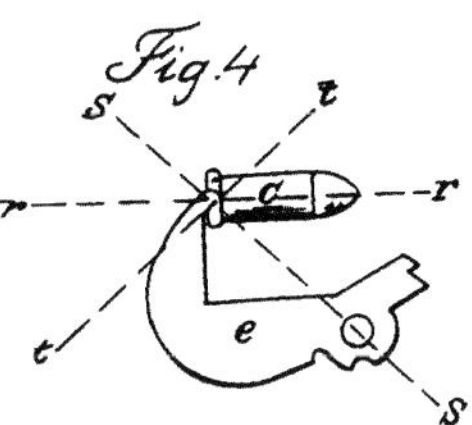

Illustration of the underslung hammer which was applied to the Remington Vest Pocket Pistols.

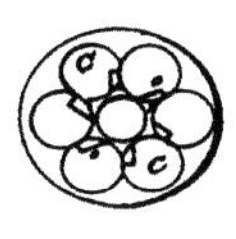

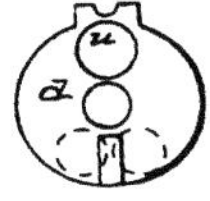

Witnesses:

S Remington
Benj P Markham

Inventor:

Wm H Elliot

Appendix 8C

Breech-Loading Fire-Arm

No. 1.663. Reissued May. 3. 1864.

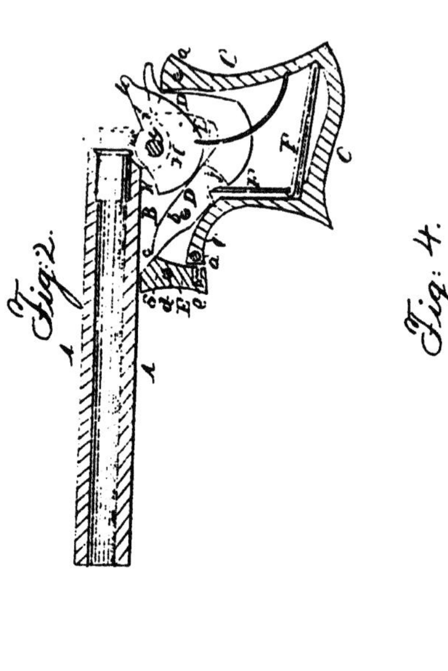

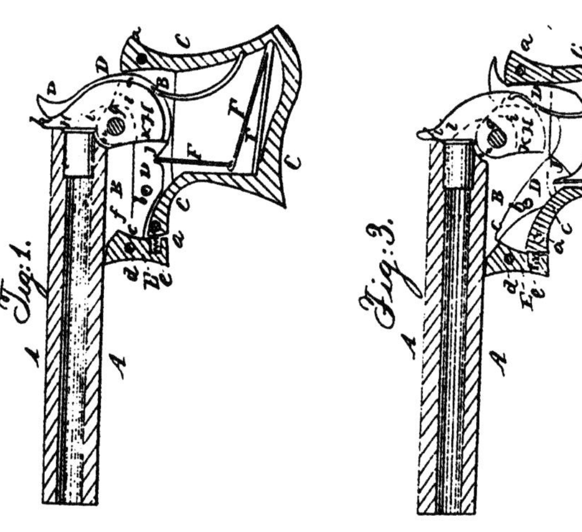

Witnesses.

Appendix 8D

J. RIDER.

Breech-Loading Fire-Arm.

No. 40.887. Patented Dec. 8, 1863.

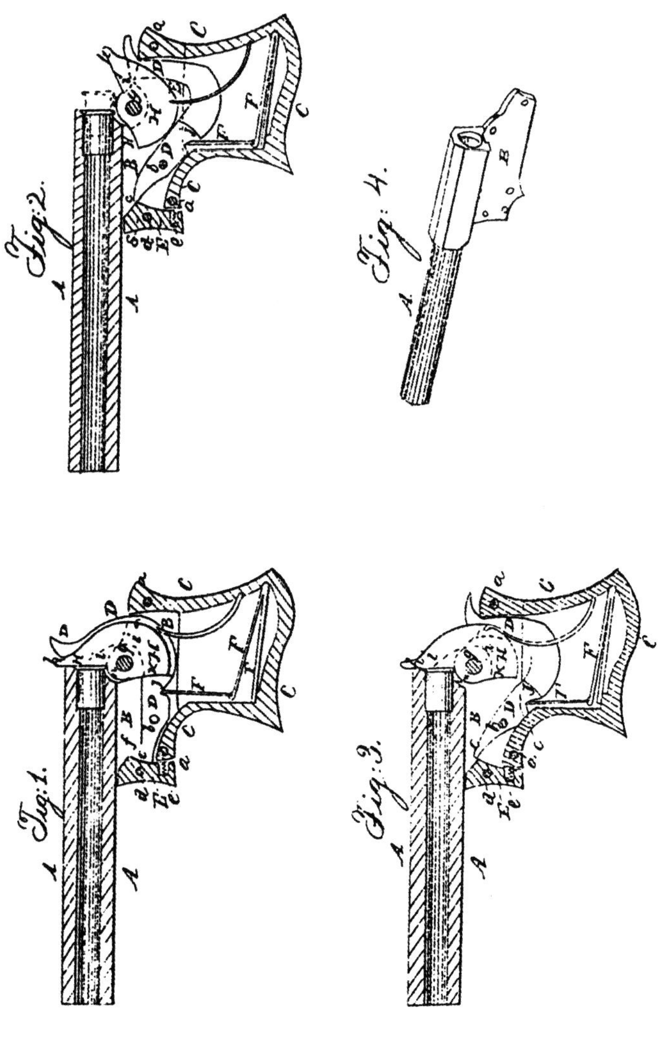

Witnesses.

Appendix 8E

J. RIDER.

Breech-Loading Fire-Arm.

No. 53,543. Patented Mar. 27, 1866.

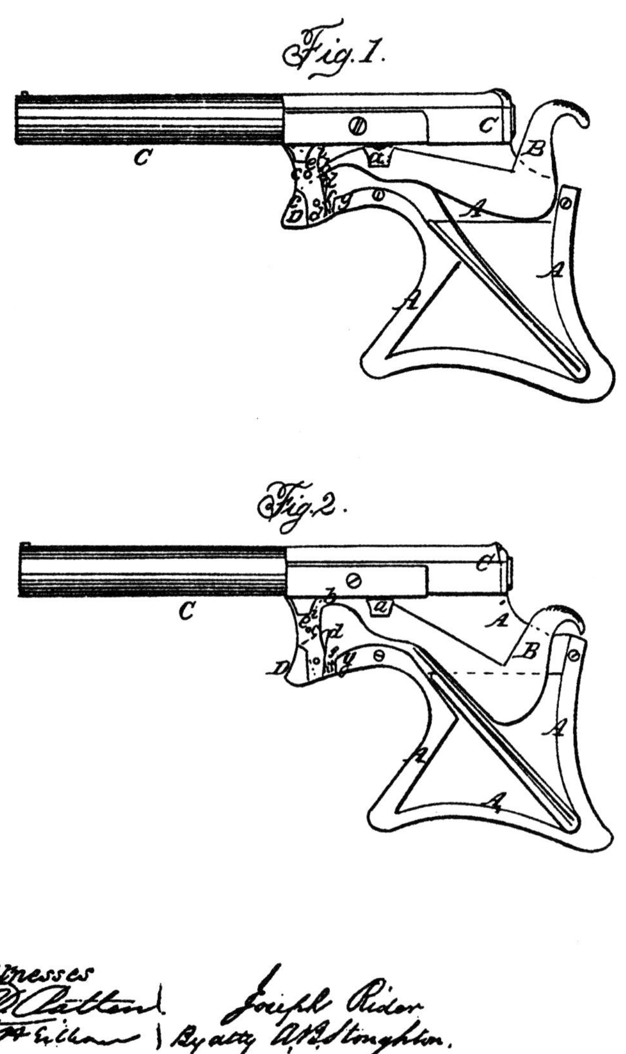

Appendix 8F

J. RIDER.

Breech-Loading Fire-Arm.

No. 45,123. **Patented Nov. 15. 1864**

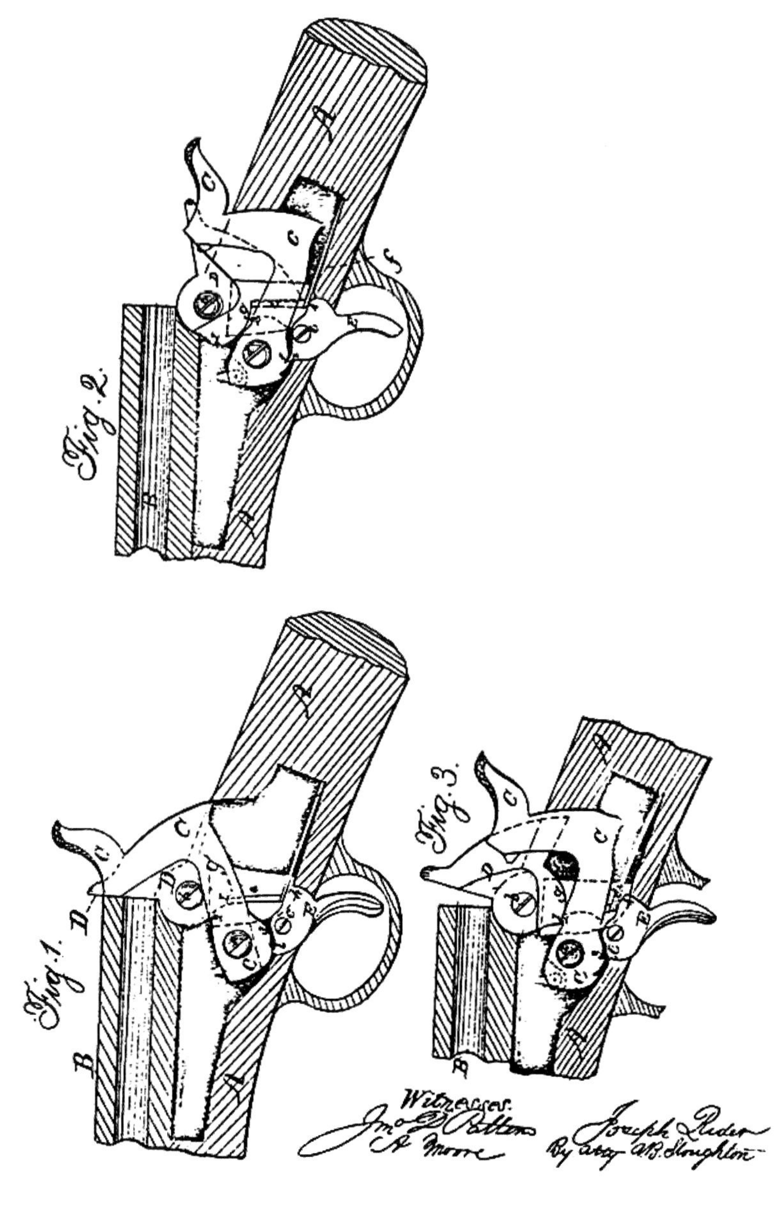

UNITED STATES PATENT OFFICE.

JOSEPH RIDER, OF NEWARK, OHIO, ASSIGNOR TO HIMSELF AND E. REMINGTON & SONS, OF ILION, NEW YORK.

IMPROVEMENT IN BREECH-LOADING FIRE-ARMS.

Specification forming part of Letters Patent No. **45,123**, dated November 15, 1864.

To all whom it may concern:

Be it known that I, JOSEPH RIDER, of Newark, in the county of Licking and State of Ohio, have invented certain new and useful Improvements in Breech-Loading Fire-Arms; and I do hereby declare that the following is a full, clear, and exact description of the same, reference being had to the accompanying drawings, making a part of this specification, in which—

Figure 1 represents a longitudinal section through the gun, and showing the breech-plate up against the bore of the gun and the hammer against or interlocked with the breech-plate. Fig. 2 represents a similar section showing the hammer at "full-cock" and the breech-plate as swung back to open the rear of the barrel to charge the gun, and both breech-piece and hammer as not only interlocked, but the trigger as being actually locked, so that it cannot be moved or release its sear or dog from its notch in the hammer. Fig. 3 represents a similar section showing the hammer at the full-cock and the breech-plate as nearly up against the bore of the gun, and showing an auxiliary or safely-locking mechanism which, although the trigger may be moved, will not allow the hammer to fly until the breech-plate is moved up still closer to or practically against the bore of the gun, and which latter mechanism would come into action should the trigger-locking device break or fail to act from any cause.

Similar letters of reference, where they occur in the separate figures, denote like parts of the arm in all the drawings.

In the patent granted to myself and E. Remington & Sons, No. 40,887, and dated 8th December, 1863, afterward reissued 3d May, 1864, and numbered 1,663, the interlocking of the breech-piece and the hammer, both when up as well as when down, is fully shown; but my present invention has for its object a more positive locking mechanism, which will not allow the hammer to fly up, so long as the bore of the gun is open, as in the act of charging the piece with a cartridge.

My invention consists in locking the hammer while the arm is being loaded, or, in other words, in locking the hammer while the bore is exposed or the breech-plate thrown back for the insertion of the cartridge.

To enable others skilled in the art to make and use my invention, I will proceed to describe the same with reference to the drawings.

A may represent the stock of the fire-arm, and B the barrel, which is bored through and through, so as to be charged at the rear.

C is the hammer, pivoted at *a*.

D is the breech-piece, hinged or pivoted at *b*, and E is the trigger, pivoted at *c*. The hammer and breech-piece are so made and arranged as to interlock with each other, as in my former invention hereinbefore referred to; and the trigger and hammer have the ordinary trigger and hammer connections with regard to each other; but I have arranged another mechanism which will lock the hammer and prevent it from flying up until the breech-plate is swung fully up against the bore of the gun, or until the trigger is pulled, as in other arms, thus preventing any premature flying of the hammer or discharging of the cartridge until the arm is to be fired. An arm, *e*, on the end of a spring-piece, *f*, stands nearly vertically under the pivot of the breech-piece D, so that when said breech-piece is swung back the portion *g* thereof will take against the top of said arm and press it and its connected portion *f* down with it until the part *f* rests against the heel *h* of the trigger and completely locks the trigger, so that it cannot be moved, and consequently its dog *i* cannot be drawn out of the full-cock notch, (which is clearly shown in Fig. 2,) nor can any premature flying up of the hammer occur so long as the breech-piece is drawn back, or until it is up, or nearly so, to the bore of the barrel, or, in other words, there is a positive locking of the hammer against any movement accidental or otherwise; but this locking is an automatic movement contingent upon the moving of the breech-piece, and is not a separate mechanism requiring a separate manipulation, which would render it almost impracticable as an army gun. This locking of the hammer in case the arm *e* should break or be removed can be effected in another way—viz., by means of the recess 1 in the breech-piece and the projection 2 on the hammer—for, suppose the arm *c* to be removed or to be broken off, as shown in Fig. 3, then the trigger could be moved and its dog release the hammer; but the hammer cannot fly up until the breech-piece is swung clear up, and this cannot be done without very great force, for when the breech-plate comes up as far as shown in Fig. 3, where it still holds the hammer interlocked, its recess 1 takes upon the projection 2 on the hammer, and there stops. Now, to draw the hammer back, so as to release the breech-piece and allow it to swing clear up to the barrel, brings it within the influence of the trigger, where it is caught on the full-cock notch 3 and held. Thus under any and all circumstances there is no danger of a premature flying up of the hammer, and only when the breech-piece is up and the hammer on the full-cock can the hammer be let off, for so long as the bore of the gun is open or the breech-piece moved back from it, so long will there be a positive locking of the hammer against any accidental flying by pulling the trigger or otherwise. I have called it "locking the hammer." It may be called "locking the trigger," as the trigger controls and lets fly the hammer under varying circumstances, and when the trigger is locked and the hammer on the full-cock of course the hammer is locked too, as the trigger cannot be moved to allow it to fly.

Having thus fully described the nature, object, and purpose of my invention, what I claim as new, and desire to secure by Letters Patent, is—

1. Locking the hammer while the arm is being loaded or the bore is exposed for the insertion of the cartridge, substantially as and for the purpose set forth.

2. An auxiliary locking mechanism consisting of the recess 1 in the breech-plate and the projection 2 on the hammer, as and for the purpose described.

JOSEPH RIDER.

Witnesses:
W. H. THOMAS,
MARSHALL LEWIS.

Appendix 9

This is a copy of a letter received from a Remington collector who has tracked Vest Pocket Pistol serial numbers for more than 30 years.

Jim Shaffer
P.O. Box 381
Irwin, PA 15642

May 30, 1997

Dear Bob:

Enclosed find many copies for your Remington Vest Pocket Pistol Survey.

1. I took your form and reduced it to fit two on a page. Hope you don't mind. Strictly a cost savings and weight savings on mailing.
2. Some things you need to include are:
   a. Brass or iron frame for the .30 cal.
   b. Rosewood for the grips.
   c. Nickel for the finish.
   d. By gilt do you mean gold plating? – not necessarily interchangeable.
3. The first pages stapled are those I own or had handy.
4. The rest are a collection of serials observed at gun shows, in catalogs, auction lists and books, notably Locke and Matthews, over the past 30+ years.
5. Most sorry, but I did not always record what you needed, careless of me, but I was not as tuned into Remington variations as I am to Marlin derringers and Stevens tip-downs. Never gave a thought to number of pins and screws in the frame. I will not make that mistake again.
6. I helped with the *Derringer Book II* with Doug Eberhart, but there are a few manufactured totals I absolutely do not agree with (I believe they are printing or transposition errors by the editor or programmer). I'll list my thoughts and opinions and let you agree or disagree. Most is based on years of observations, with several others, of the most pertinent details: i.e.;
7. a. I believe that all calibers were numbered in their own sequence starting at serial No. 1.
   b. I do not believe that a .38 was ever made, Too powerful for the split-breech – .38 rimfire kicks like a mule.
   c. I believe that the brass frame .30 cal. is about half of production in .30 cal.
   d. I do not believe the .32 was ever produced in brass. (I could be mistaken on this one).
   e. Rosewood grips are a lot more common than 20%. Most people cannot tell walnut from rosewood. Rosewood is usually dark, multi-colored with soft yellows, reds, orange, tans and dark browns. Walnut (except deluxe) is usually light/medium-colored with grain.
   f. I don't believe silver is second to nickel. I'd list it as: nickel, blue, silver then gold. But .41s seem to be more blued than nickel.
   g. I believe the production figures are as follows:

- .22 cal. About 15,000 – 65 recorded from 3 to 16824 (however there is a high serial number of 16824. Eng., gold, ivory, but it is from a Jackson catalog and is not confirmed. The nearest serial number to it is 14,379. That's 2,500 away. Too big a gap. From a total 65 numbers.
- .30 cal. About 2,800 – 18 examined – 7 brass frames – 11 iron frames (however there is a high serial number of 7,688 on a British proofed & marked one. This is suspect, as the nearest high number is 2681. No way!
- .32 cal. About 3,000 or 3,500+/- (But with a possible 3,500 to 4,000) – Only 12 recorded, from 191 to 3515 – but nearest is 2794. Highest number is a 10-inch stocked one at No. 3513 which may represent the high end as they experimented with leftover frames. Just a guess.
- .41 cal. About 5,000 – 32 recorded from 13 to 4812 – In *Derringer II*, this is a long way from 14,000 given as a total. I have no idea where that quantity came from, as I have all Doug's serial data. If that were the case, they would turn up with the frequency of the .22 – They definitely do not.

Total Observed – all calibers: 127

So, a grand total of all calibers somewhere between 25,800 to 28,300+/-. All subjective, of course, and remember "in Gun collecting there are no absolutes!!" Now, the job is to fill in the missing numbers. Hope this helps, keep in touch, bounce a few theories off my skull, etc. and, of course Good Luck!

P.S. I've studied Marlin Derringers for 35 years and have recorded 300 serial numbers. Still no absolute conclusions. Marlin numbers are all over the place. I think Remington is a lot easier.

Best,
JIM

P.P.S. – If you do not have the Doug Eberhart serial numbers, I'll be happy to send them to you. I've only enclosed mine. Would appreciate your keeping me updated on your findings. As I find additional data, I'll send it on.

Bibliography

Balderson, Robert H. (1996). *The Official Price Guide to Antique and Modern Firearms*, 8th Edition, House of Collectibles, NY.

Ball, Robert W.D. (1995). *Remington Firearms: The Golden Age of Collecting*. Krause Publications, Iola, WI.

Bannerman Military Goods Catalogue (1940). Francis Bannerman & Sons, 501 Broadway, NY.

Bourne, Richard A. (1980). *The Remington Collection of Karl Moldenhauer*. Richard A. Bourne Company, Inc., Hyannis, Mass.

Bowman, Hank Wieand (1953). *Antique Guns* (ed. Lucian Cary). A Fawcett Book No. 209; (1964). *Antique Guns from the Stagecoach Collection*, A Fawcett Book No. 577; Fawcett Publications, Greenwich, Conn.

Eberhart, L.D. and R.L. Wilson (1993). *The Deringer in America. Vol. II, The Cartridge Period*. Andrew Mowbray Publishers, Inc., Lincoln, RI.

Faintich Auction Services, Inc., Catalogs, (1996–1999).

Fjestad, S.P. (1994). *Blue Book of Gun Values 15th Edition*. Blue Book Publications, Inc., Minneapolis, Minn.

Flayderman, Norm (1994). *Flayderman's Guide to Antique American Firearms* 6th Edition. DBI Books, Inc., Northbrook, Ill.

Gun Journal (June 1997), pg. 71; (Oct. 1997), pg. 69; (Feb. 1998), pg. 85.

Hatch, Alden (1956). *Remington Arms in American History*. Clarke, Irwin & Co. LTD., Toronto, Canada.

Hatfield, Robert (1997). *Remington Vest Pocket Pistols and the Celebrated Saw-Handle-Grip Pocket Pistol*. Hatfield, LTD., Lake Ozark, MO.; (1999) *A Continuing Story…*, pg. 42, *Remington Society of America Journal*, (2nd quarter 1999).

Karr, Charles Lee, Jr.; Karr, Caroll Robbins (1960). *Remington Handguns*. Second Edition, Stackpole Publishing, Harrisburg, Penn.

Kirkland, K.D. (1988). *American Premier Gunmakers: Remington*. Bison Books Corp., Hong Kong.

Larson, E. Dixon (1975). *Remington Tips*. Pioneer Press, Nashville, Tenn.

Madaus, Howard M. and Simeon Stoddard (1997). *The Guns of Remington*, Biplane Productions, Cobb, Inc., Dayton, KY.

Man at Arms magazine, (Vol. 20, No. 1), Jan. 1998, pg. 46, Book Review. Andrew Mowbray Publishers, Inc., Lincoln, RI.

Marcot, Roy (1998). *Remington, America's Oldest Gunmaker*. Primedia, Special Interest Publications, Peoria, IL.

Moody, L.W. (1992). *Machinist*, Advertising Brochure — "The Remington-Rider Parlor Pistol" — Alum Bridge, WV.

Museum of Historical Arms, Catalog #15 (1963).

Peterson, Harold (1966). *The Remington Historical Treasury of American Guns*. Gossett and Dunlap, New York.

Remington Catalogs and Sales Brochures, (1865–1888).

Rock Island Auction Company, Catalogs (1992–1999).

Schwing, Ned and Herb Houze (1996). *Standard Catalog of Firearms,* Sixth Edition. Krause Publications, Iola, WI.

Sellers, Frank M. (1973). *The William M. Locke Collection*. Antique Armory, Inc., East Point, Georgia.

Serven, James E. (ed.) (1996). *The Collecting of Guns*. Crown Publishers, New York.

Supica, Jim and Eve (1998). Old Town Station Dispatch #20, Old Town Station, LTD., Lenexa, KS.

Time-Life (ed.) (1997 Reissue edition). *The Gamblers* (Old West), pg. 147. Time-Life Books.

West, Bill (1970). *Remington Arms and History,* First Edition. Stockton-Doty Trade Press, Whittier, CA. Remington Arms Catalogs, 1877–1899.

Wier, Leon, *Remington Society of America Journal*. (April 1991), pg. 4; (1994, First Quarter), "Rem Shots," pgs. 4 and 5; (1996, Third Quarter), "Rem Shots," pgs. 4–6; (1999, Third Quarter), pg. 5.

World Book Encyclopedia (1998), World Book, Inc., Chicago, IL.

Acknowledgments

The author wishes to express his heartfelt gratitude to all those who responded to the requests for information and assistance. If the names of everyone (hundreds of them) who responded to those requests and the names of all of the people who volunteered their assistance were listed herein, the space requirement would probably exceed the contents of this book.

So, I would like to express my gratitude collectively to all of the Remington collectors, especially the members of the Remington Society of America, who participated. They are the greatest.

A special thank you to the authors listed in the bibliography. Their research, shared knowledge, vision, assumptions and conclusions constitute a major portion of existing firearm knowledge. Encouragement and well-wishes received from many renowned firearms authors and experts accelerated the pace and helped compound the scope of this endeavor.

Additional thanks to those authors who volunteered the use of their data and photographs.

The encouragement and input from interested collectors around the world provided the necessary catalyst to keep the project moving.

The indulgence of museum curators and their employees must also be publicly applauded.

The staff at the McCracken Research Library, Buffalo Bill Historical Center, Cody, WY, have earned my respect and gratitude. Their assistance and cooperation gave this book a real shot in the arm, just prior to the 1997 RSA Meeting conducted at the center.

A first-class "ATTA-BOY and Appreciation Award" goes to my valued friend and computer guru Jim Bivins. Without his knowledge, computer skills, encouragement, suggestions, prodding and proofreading, this book would still be in the "Some day I'm gonna…" stage. For a guy who doesn't collect Remingtons, Jim is all right!

Then there's Leon Wier, Jr. (Ol' RemShots). If Leon had not suggested that I try my hand at Vest Pocket research, this book would never have been started. His responses, that I am aware of, to inquiries concerning Vest Pockets are listed in the bibliography. Leon's encouragement, counsel and assistance played a major role in getting this study going and stimulating completion.

Roy Marcot, editor of the *Remington Society of America Journal*, provided assistance no other could have. His inclusion of the Vest Pocket Pistol research survey forms with *RSA Journal* distributions really got the ball rolling on this project. His suggestions and encouragement will never be forgotten.

There are so many who unselfishly provided their knowledge, assistance, research information, photographs and illustrations. People like Fritz Baehr, John Battaglia, Elliott L. Burka, Charles Doty, Doug Eberhart, Herbert Houze, Jay Huber, Bill Lawrence, Dick Littlefield, J. Wayne Matthews, L.W. Moody, Stuart Mowbray, Jim Shaffer, Don Williams and E.J. Williams. Gentlemen, thank you all.

To Pat Hogan and all the folks at Rock Island (Illinois) Auction Company, thank you for all your kindnesses to me personally and for your generous contribution of the complete set of your gun auction catalogs for future research to the Remington Society of America.

The late Jeff Faintich, Faintich Auction (St. Louis), donated a set of Faintich Auction Catalogs to the Remington Society of America to aid future researchers. Thanks, Jeff.

I apologize for my failing memory for any omission of supporters who came to my rescue. Please accept my apologies and profound gratitude for every assistance given.

To my family members and friends that I have virtually ignored during the pursuit of completion of this book, I can only say, Thank You for your support and encouragement. Please accept my apologies.

Index